AIRFARE SECRETS EXPOSED

How to Find the Lowest Fares
Available Anywhere!

Third Edition

Joel Leach and Carey Christensen

Studio 4 Productions
Northridge, CA

Studio 4 Productions
Post Office Box 280400
Northridge, CA 91328-0400
© 1994, 1998, 2000 by Studio 4 Productions
All rights reserved. First Edition 1994
Third Edition 2000
Printed in the United States of America

Library of Congress Catalog Card Number: 99-72794

ISBN: 1-882349-18-0

Book Design: Carey Christensen

Cover Design: Bob Aulicino

Printed by: Patterson Printing, Benton Harbor, MI

TABLE OF CONTENTS

Acknowledgments v

Warning/Disclaimer vi

Introduction vii

CHAPTER 1
Consolidators, Bucket Shops,
and Discounters Offer Bargain Airfare 1

CHAPTER 2
Airline Ticket Auctions—
A New Way to Buy Airline Tickets 19

CHAPTER 3
Air Courier Savings 21

CHAPTER 4
Air Passes—Bargain Prices "Over There" 51

CHAPTER 5
Status Fares—Savings for Being Someone Special 57

CHAPTER 6
Budget Travel via the Internet 61

CHAPTER 7
Charter Airlines Offer Savings 67

CHAPTER 8
Good Timing = Big $aving$! 69

CHAPTER 9
Get Bumped—Get Ca$h! 73

CHAPTER 10
Maximize Your Frequent Flyer Earnings 79

CHAPTER 11
Tips, Tricks, and Secrets 93

APPENDIX 1
Travel Resources Recommended by the Authors 103

APPENDIX 2
Travel Advisories and Emergency Assistance 113

APPENDIX 3
Travel Insurance 117

APPENDIX 4
Non-Fare-Related Travel Tips 121

APPENDIX 5
For the Disabled Traveler 125

APPENDIX 6
Passports and Visas 131

APPENDIX 7
Foreign Entry Requirements 137

APPENDIX 8
Airline Telephone Numbers and Internet Addresses 167

APPENDIX 9
Airport Codes 185

Acknowledgments

The authors would like to thank Matt and Sharon Wunder, friends and travel junkies whose efforts gave birth to the first edition of **Airfare Secrets Exposed.**

WARNING/DISCLAIMER

This book was written to educate, entertain and provide information only on the subject matter covered. It is sold with the understanding that the publisher and the author are not engaged in rendering legal, accounting or other professional services. If legal or other expert assistance is required, the services of a competent professional should be sought.

The authors and *Studio 4 Productions* shall have neither liability nor responsibility to any person with respect to loss or damage caused, or alleged to be caused, directly or indirectly by the information contained in this book.

Although the authors and publisher have made every effort to ensure that the information contained in the book is correct and current, the authors and publisher do not assume and hereby disclaim any liability to any party for any loss or damage caused by errors or omissions, or any potential travel disruption due to labor or financial difficulty, whether such errors or omissions result from negligence, accident, or any other cause.

INTRODUCTION

Congratulations on taking your first step toward learning how to save money each and every time you fly!

For Individuals and for Businesses, too!

If you're an individual who takes just three cross-country trips a year, you'll be able to shave $1,200 or more off the airlines' published fares—just like the authors themselves have done over and over again!

And, if you own a business and your employees take just a moderate number of trips annually, you'll be able to reduce travel expenses by $10,000-$15,000 or more, instantly! And what business doesn't need to reduce costs?

Save on Both Domestic and International Flights

The secrets contained in this book are universal. That means you'll save when flying to visit grandma and grandpa in Norfolk and you'll save even more when you fly to visit Rome and Athens in Europe!

You'll save so much that soon, you'll be able to travel to exotic lands you thought you would *never* see!

It's All Legal!

Each chapter contains money-saving TIPS, TRICKS, AND SECRETS THAT THE AIRLINES WISH YOU DIDN'T KNOW! And the best part is that *everything* the authors tell you is legal, but only known to only to those who have done their homework...those who know how the industry operates and how to beat the airlines at their own game!

Airlines Want Your Money—
You Earned it, so Why Not Keep it?

Airlines are in business to make money and they do that by charging as much as they think you're willing to pay.

But you work hard for your money and you owe it to yourself to pay as little as you possibly can.

That's where *Airfare Secrets Exposed* comes in! The authors have dug deep inside the airline industry and learned how the airlines think and how they operate—and how to turn that knowledge into SAVINGS.

Who Reads *Airfare Secrets Exposed*?

You'll be surprised; we certainly were!

We anticipated that our readership would consist mainly of fixed income people who found air travel to be too costly. Instead, we learned that our readership consists of almost equal portions of two very different groups: those who can't travel unless they can find low prices and those who are financially secure and don't need to worry about how much they pay!

So then, why are financially secure people so enthusiastic about saving money on airfare? The answer is simple: obtaining the cheapest airfare is considered an art form and a thinking person's way of competing in unfamiliar territory.

We have heard from dozens of people who have purchased our book. The common thread among our readership is a certain indescribably victorious feeling when they know the passenger sitting next to them paid three times the amount they did!

The publisher is confident that if you read **Airfare Secrets Exposed**, you'll be able to outthink the airlines and save money each and every time you fly!

CONSOLIDATORS, BUCKET SHOPS, AND DISCOUNTERS OFFER BARGAIN AIRFARES

Airline officials realize that some seats on most flights may not sell. And that translates to lost revenue.

So, in order to sell more seats, airlines often take the anticipated number of empty seats and sell them off in bulk at a cost considerably below their published fare.

The company that buys these tickets then marks them up and sells them to the public or to other travel agencies. The public gets a great deal, the airlines benefit by selling seats that might otherwise have gone unsold and of course, the agency makes money as well.

A company that buys tickets in bulk and then resells them is called a *consolidator*. Consolidators are the travel industry equivalent of warehouse retail stores that offer low prices, limited selection and minimal service.

As in most industries, market forces dictate both availability and price of a consolidator ticket. The original ticket price, the state of the economy, and the demand for the particular destination and competition, all play a role in how full or empty a particular flight might be and thus, how many consolidator tickets an airline might choose to make available.

The season also plays a role. *Off seasons* (which vary depending upon proximity to the equator), generally mean lost revenue for airlines. During off-seasons, airlines are more likely to sell tickets to consolidators.

Airlines are reluctant to admit they sell tickets to consolidators, who in turn make them available to the public at lower prices than the airlines themselves offer. This is because airlines believe that if their regular passengers were to learn that airline tickets were available at such low prices elsewhere, they would expect the airlines to offer the same low rate as well. But in reality, even if you call a ticket agent or regular travel agent and ask for the airline's *very best deal,* they are often unable to compete with consolidator prices!

It is worth noting that in recent years, a number of airlines have even set up their own in-house consolidating businesses. Of course, such an operation always uses a different name than that of the airline with which it is affiliated.

Bucket Shops

The term "Bucket Shop" originated in London in the 1970s when the airlines were looking for a way to make discounted seats available on the marketplace without seeming to be involved. Airlines sold tickets to bucket shops that would then sell them to the public at discounted rates.

In actuality, Europe's bucket shops have a great deal in common with airline ticket consolidators in the U.S.—so much so that the terms are often used interchangeably although technical differences still remain (among other things, bucket shops also buy only from one another while consolidators buy from the airline.)

The truth is that airline ticket discounters, wanting to maximize their presence, have begun referring to themselves as both *consolidators* and *bucket shops*. So, it is always wise to enter both terms when you go Internet shopping for discounted airline tickets.

Safety in Buying

Most consolidators are legitimate but some are not. For that reason, it's best that you use the services of consolidators recommended by friends. You can also ask whether a consolidator belongs to the American Society of Travel Agents, a trade group whose members are bound by a code of ethics.

Consolidators sometimes also belong to the Airlines Reporting Corporation, a group that accredits agencies to sell airline tickets. ARC members must prove that they meet financial and legal requirements as demanded by the airlines. It's worth noting however, that ARC is an arm of the airlines themselves; it is not a consumer protection organization.

You might also want to check with the Better Business Bureau, as membership there implies a good-faith intention to resolve consumer disputes.

Buy Insurance to Protect Your Airline Ticket Purchase

The purchasing of travel insurance to support your discount ticket purchase is a wise idea. The discount agency isn't likely to offer travel insurance (ask to be sure), but you can buy it from The American Automobile Association (AAA) and other sources (see appendix).

Insurance averages about 4-5% of the value of an airline ticket. Such insurance will protect you if a consolidator, airline or even a travel agency goes bankrupt or vanishes before your departure date. (See Appendix 3 for Travel Insurance information.)

Consolidator Ratings

The *Index to Air Travel Consolidators* published by Travel Publishing of Oakdale, Minnesota (800/241-9299) rates consolidators. However, it doesn't list *all* consolidators and it includes many that sell only to travel agents.

Excellent Savings

There is no established formula that indicates how much you'll save by buying your airline tickets from a consolidator because consolidators price tickets according to supply and demand. However, during peak season travel when ticket prices are high, you can expect to save 20-50%.

Usually, consolidators charge just a little more than half of a round trip fare if the customer wants a one-way ticket. (Airlines generally charge *much* more). Tickets that need to be "dumped" because of an impending departure with unsold seats are often sold for pennies on the dollar.

Other Considerations

Consolidator tickets offer great savings, but they are not always available and typically, they carry a number of restrictions.

Also, discount tickets sometimes do not qualify for advanced seat selection, so it is possible that you might end up with what you might consider to be a less-than-desirable seat. This is not the case with most consolidator tickets, however.

Generally, consolidator tickets are only good for the issuing airline. So if you miss a flight or your flight is delayed, your ticket probably won't be honored on another airline.

Also, some airlines do not accept tickets bought through consolidators for their frequent flyer programs.

Consolidator Ticket Restrictions

Consolidator/discount tickets generally have "non-refundable" written on them, because they usually have the regular fare printed on them rather than the price you paid. Sometimes they display no fare at all). After all, airlines don't want you to return your ticket for a profit. So, if you must cancel your flight and you want a refund, you'll have to go through the consolidator and/or his agent.

However, a consolidator ticket will often have fewer restrictions on it than will a promotional fare issued by an airline. So sometimes, when the price of the consolidator ticket and the promotional ticket is the same, it might well be wise to buy the consolidator ticket.

Before you complete your ticket order with a consolidator, verify total price (including taxes and fees), ticket delivery date, restrictions, cancellation policy, and the name and delivery address. It can be both difficult and costly to make corrections later.

Classes of Service

Most discount tickets are for coach (economy) class seats, although you can occasionally find tickets in other classes as well. First Class and Business Class prices are not as great a bargain, however.

You cannot generally upgrade a discount ticket by paying a surcharge. However, if the regular fare is printed on the ticket (rather than what you paid or just the tax), you might be able to do so. Give it a try.

Finding a Consolidator or Ticket Discounter

Below, we have listed discount ticket sellers by state. Some, but not all, are consolidators.

We urge you not to limit yourself to calling only those discounters located near you.. That is because discounters do not all have the same tickets or prices available—in fact, discounters buy different quantities of tickets at different prices and that affects what each will be able to make available to you as well. So it is strongly suggested that you make multiple calls in order to locate the a price and schedule that best suits your needs.

It is worth also noting that some consolidators deal only with travel agents, and not the general public.

Also, some consolidators are dedicated exclusively to domestic flights while others focus on international flights. Some handle both.

You have a choice: You may wish to call the consolidators yourself or, if you prefer, contact a travel agent who will search for a consolidator ticket for you. *Keep in mind, however, that many travel agents do not offer consolidator tickets.* Also, remember that a travel agent will most likely tack on a fee for his services.

Yet another source for consolidator tickets is your newspaper's Sunday travel section. Unfortunately, not all consolidators listed in newspapers are legitimate. It is possible that you could end up buying a stolen and/or an unauthorized ticket. So beware!

Buying Consolidator Tickets from Travel Agents

Some travel agents sell consolidator tickets; however, travel agents usually work with a short list of consolidators so they won't know everything that is available out there.

The good part about using the services of a travel agent is that he has more leverage than you do and may even cover your loss if the consolidator declares bankruptcy. However, you should be aware of the fact that a travel agent will generally tack on a service fee that can be as much as $50 per ticket.

Buying Consolidator Tickets on the Internet

A growing list of Internet travel agencies claim they have access to low fares from all sources, including consolidators. Most, however, access only some consolidators, not all, so be sure to search multiple sources.

Paying for Your Ticket

Always use your charge card when purchasing an airline ticket from a discounter. Then, if the transaction doesn't go as you expected, at least you can ask the credit card company for a refund.

Warning!

If the consolidator will not guarantee delivery of your ticket within a week or two, find another consolidator. Exceptional delays can mean that the company is financially unstable.

If your ticket doesn't arrive when the seller promised, call the airline on which the consolidator booked you to confirm that you actually have a reservation. If you're not ticketed, call the consolidator and cancel. If the consolidator refuses to cooperate, call your credit card company and file a dispute.

Consolidator/Discounter Directory

Following, is a list of agencies that sell discount tickets. Some, but not all, are consolidators. They offer tickets to various destinations around the world. If one agency doesn't have the ticket you want, then call another.

The following agencies collectively sell airplane tickets to Africa, Asia, Caribbean, Central America, Europe, Hawaii, Middle East, North America, South America and the South Pacific.

Arizona

Cheap Seats	800/451-7200
Cheap Tickets	800/377-1000
Council Travel	800/226-8624

Northern California

Air Brokers International	800/883-3273
Airbound	415/834-9445
Budget Traveler	415/331-3700

Cheap Seats	800/451-7200
Cheap Tickets	800/377-1000
China Travel Service	800/899-8618
Council Travel S.F	800/226-8624
Custom Travel	800/535-9797
Festival of Asia	800/533-9953
Pioneer Tours	800/288-2107
Scan the World	415/325-0876
Skytours	800/246-8687
STA Travel	800/777-0112
Sun Destination Travel	415/398-1313
Sundance Travel	415/677-0799
Travel Design Unlimited	415/969-2000
Vacation Land	800/245-0050

Southern California

All Continents Travel	800/368-6822
Bi-Coastal Travel	800/926-2782
	310/649-2326
The Bucket Shop	310/641-5354
Cheap Seats	800/451-7200
Cheap Tickets	800/377-1000
C.L. Thomson Thrifty Air	800/833-4258
Continental Travel Shop	310/453-8655
Council Travel	800/226-8624
Discount Air Network	888/624-7327
Discover Wholesale Travel	800/576-7770
Euram Flight Center	800/555-3872
Fare Deal Travel	619/298-8869

Flight Coordinators	800/544-3644
K&K Travel	800/523-1374
Levon Travel	800/445-3866
Sita World Travel	818/767-0039
Southern Connections	800/635-3303
South Star Tours	800/654-4468
STA Travel	800/777-0112

Colorado

Cheap Seats	800/451-7200
Cheap Tickets	800/377-1000
Council Travel	800/226-8624
Elias Travel	800/303-5427
Overseas Travel	800/783-7196

Connecticut

All Destinations	800/228-1510
Cheap Seats	800/451-7200
Cheap Tickets	800/377-1000
Council Travel	800/226-8624
Tread Lightly	800/643-0060

District of Columbia

Cheap Seats	800/451-7200
Cheap Tickets	800/377-1000
Council Travel	800/226-8624
Democracy Travel	800/536-8728
EURAM Flight Center	800/775-2299
STA Travel	800/777-0112

Florida

Arnsdorff Travel Agency	407/886-1343
Cheap Seats	800/451-7200
Cheap Tickets	800/377-1000
Cosmopolitan Travel Center	800/548-7206
Council Travel	800/226-8624
Direct Line Travel & Cruises	800/422-2585
EURAM Flight Center	954/455-9904
Interworld	800/468-3796
	305/443-4929
The Smart Traveler	800/448-3338
STA Travel	800/777-0112

Georgia

Alpha Travel	800/793-8424
Cheap Seats	800/451-7200
Cheap Tickets	800/377-1000
Council Travel	800/226-8624
Midtown Travel	800/548-8904

Illinois

Chisolm Travel	800/631-2824
Cheap Seats	800/451-7200
Cheap Tickets	800/377-1000
Council Travel	800/226-8624
Cut Rate Travel	800/388-0575
Greaves Travel	800/473-2837
Malaysia Travel Advisors	888/359-8655
Mena Tours & Travel	800/937-6362

STA Travel	800/777-0112
Travel Avenue	800/333-3335
Travel Core of America	800/992-9396
Unlimited World Travel	800/322-3557

Indiana

Cheap Seats	800/451-7200
Cheap Tickets	800/377-1000
Council Travel	800/226-8624

Iowa

Cheap Seats	800/451-7200
Cheap Tickets	800/377-1000
Council Travel	800/226-8624

Kansas

Cheap Seats	800/451-7200
Cheap Tickets	800/377-1000
Council Travel	800/226-8624

Louisiana

Cheap Seats	800/451-7200
Cheap Tickets	800/377-1000
Council Travel	800/226-8624

Maine

Cheap Seats	800/451-7200
Cheap Tickets	800/377-1000
Council Travel	800/226-8624

Destination Europe	800/223-5555

Maryland

AESU Travel	800/638-7640
Cheap Seats	800/451-7200
Cheap Tickets	800/377-1000
Council Travel	800/226-8624
Fare Deals	800/347-7006
Hans World Travel	800/421-4267

Massachusetts

Cheap Seats	800/451-7200
Cheap Tickets	800/377-1000
Council Travel	800/226-8624
Spector Travel	800/879-2374
STA Travel	800/777-0112

Michigan

Cheap Seats	800/451-7200
Cheap Tickets	800/377-1000
Council Travel	800/226-8624
Greaves Travel	800/473-2837
GTI Travel Consolidators	800/829-8234

Minnesota

Cheap Seats	800/451-7200
Cheap Tickets	800/377-1000
Council Travel	612/379-2323
Travel Ways	800/876-3131

Missouri

Airfare Hotline	800/455-2359
Cheap Seats	800/451-7200
Cheap Tickets	800/377-1000
Council Travel	612/379-2323
Group & Leisure Travel	800/874-6608

New Jersey

British Network	800/274-8583
Cheap Seats	800/451-7200
Cheap Tickets	800/377-1000
Council Travel	612/379-2323
Garden State Travel	201333-1232
Paul Laifer Tours	800/346-6314
Rupa Travel Services	800/572-5001
Worldvision Travel Services	800/545-7118

New York

Air Travel Discounts	800/888-2621
Asensio Tours & Travel	800/221-7679
Balkan Holidays	800/822-1106
Calcos Tours	800/338-2288
Cheap Seats	800/451-7200
Cheap Tickets	800/377-1000
Council Travel	800/226-8624
Fantasy Holidays	800/645-2555
Favored Holidays	718/934-8881
French Experience	212/986-3800
Greaves Travel	800/473-2837

Homeric tours	800/223-5570
Magical Holidays	800/228-2208
New Frontiers	800/366-6387
Oxford Travel	800/425-9958
Pharos Travel & Tourism	800/999-5511
Pino Welcome Travel	800/247-6578
STA Travel	800/777-0112
TFI Tours	800/745-8000
Travel Center	800/419-0960
Travel 'N Tours	800/984-9075
Tulips Travel	800/882-3383
United Tours	800/245-0203
Valentino Travel Service	800/457-2260

North Carolina

Cheap Seats	800/451-7200
Cheap Tickets	800/377-1000
Council Travel	800/226-8624

Ohio

Cheap Seats	800/451-7200
Cheap Tickets	800/377-1000
Council Travel	800/226-8624

Oregon

Cheap Seats	800/451-7200
Cheap Tickets	800/377-1000
Council Travel	800/226-8624

Pennsylvania

Cheap Seats	800/451-7200
Cheap Tickets	800/377-1000
Council Travel	800/226-8624
Pennsylvania Travel	800/331-0947
STA/University Travel	800/777-0112

Rhode Island

Cheap Seats	800/451-7200
Cheap Tickets	800/377-1000
Council Travel	800/226-8624

Tennessee

Cheap Seats	800/451-7200
Cheap Tickets	800/377-1000
Council Travel	800/226-8624

Texas

Carefree Getaway Travel	800/969-8687
Cheap Seats	800/451-7200
Cheap Tickets	800/377-1000
Council Travel	800/226-8624
Embassy Tours	800/299-5284
Royal Lane Travel	800/329-2030

Utah

Cheap Seats	800/451-7200
Cheap Tickets	800/377-1000
Council Travel	800/226-8624

Virginia

Cheap Seats	800/451-7200
Cheap Tickets	800/377-1000
Council Travel	800/226-8624
Fellowship Travel International	800/235-9384

Washington, D.C.

Americas Tours & Travel	800/553-2513
Cheap Seats	800/451-7200
Cheap Tickets	800/377-1000
Council Travel	800/226-8624
Americas Tours	800/553-2513
STA Travel	800/777-0112

Canada

Connections Travel	800/663-2293
Payless Travel	416/922-2667
TEC Travel	800/335-5641
Travel Air	800/335-2304
Travel Cuts	800/667-2887
Voyages Performance	514/282-1022

Two Internet addresses that claim to have access to all consolidator fares are:

Economytravel.com
http://www.economytravel.com

1travel.com
http://www1travel.com

And finally, a source on the Internet that claims to list all discount airfares:

http://www.advocacy-net.com/discairmks.htm

2

AIRLINE TICKET AUCTIONS— A NEW WAY TO BUY AIRLINE TICKETS

Airline ticket auctions are relatively new inventions and operate much like any other auction—you state the amount you would like to pay to fly to a particular destination and the auction house responds as to whether an airline will accept your bid or not. *Priceline.com* is probably the best known source for this service at the present time.

Remember that airlines want to make as much money as possible, so ridiculously low bids are seldom successful.

You should also know that while you are able to specify your destination and desired date of departure, the airlines select the *time* of day for your flights. And as you would expect, the flights available tend to be those that are somewhat less desirable.

Nonetheless, auctions offer yet another potential for considerable savings.

Auction Directory

There are an increasing number of web sites that offer airline fare auctions. The authors have listed their favorites below in alphabetical order:

All Shops Travel Auction
http://www.allshops.com/Travel/Air_Travel/Air_Travel_Auctions/

Bid 4 Travel
http://www.bid4travel.com

Onsale
http://www.onsale.com/departments/vacations.htm

Priceline.com
http://travel.priceline.com

SkyAuction.com
http://www.skyauction.com

Travel Bids
http://www.travelbids.com

3

AIR COURIER SAVINGS

Incredible Savings!

You can expect to save 20-50% or more on most courier flights. And fares as low as $100 round-trip are not unheard of, and sometimes, flights are actually free!

Actual savings depend on the desirability, destination, and competition on the route. And as one might expect, courier fares fluctuate with the seasons.

Courier Companies

Courier companies are wholesale or retail firms responsible for handling express shipping on a contractual basis for major air freight forwarders and express companies. Simply put, courier companies guarantee the safe and timely delivery of shipments. In order to accomplish their mission, they seek the services of *air couriers* (also known as *free lance air couriers* or simply *couriers*).

Air Courier

In the simplest terms, a courier is a person who accompanies time-sensitive business cargo checked as passenger baggage on international flights.

Couriers are not considered employees of the companies for which they travel; they are considered independent contractors. That means that the companies have limited legal responsibility for the couriers themselves.

Note: Before you sign on to serve as a courier, be sure to ask for a printed definition of their responsibilities to you and yours to them.

"The Courier Type"

All kinds of people from all walks of life fly as couriers. Students, retirees, and teachers have flexible lifestyles that make them likely candidates. But you'll also find that courier travel appeals to business owners, entrepreneurs, adventure travelers, travel writers, and many others.

Why Do Businesses Use Couriers?

All shipments to foreign countries must clear customs upon landing. Passengers with baggage are processed immediately upon landing whereas *unaccompanied* cargo is processed (inspected) *whenever customs officials can get to it*. That means that more often than not, unaccompanied cargo is unloaded from the plane and taken directly to a customs warehouse—where it might stay for hours or days awaiting processing.

There is yet another risk that faces unaccompanied cargo in certain foreign countries. Warehoused cargo—including that which is stored in "secure" customs facilities—sometimes mysteriously disappears, even from behind locked doors.

So all things considered, couriers offer both timeliness and a level of security that isn't otherwise available. In today's fast-paced world, the service offered by air couriers is considered extremely valuable.

What Does a Courier Actually Do?

A courier company purchases an economy ticket on a commercial airline, then uses the courier's luggage allowance for the shipment of their customer's cargo—and uses the courier to accompany that cargo on the flight. The courier, who in turn pays a heavily discounted rate for his airplane ticket, is permitted to spend some time on his own upon arrival at the foreign destination.

In other words, the cargo is treated like it is the courier's personal baggage. Of course, that means that the courier may be required to forfeit some or nearly all of his personal baggage space.

Depending on its size and level of security, the cargo the courier accompanies may ride in the belly of the plane, in the overhead baggage compartment or on the courier's lap.

Types of Materials Transported

You may be asked to carry a small package that fits easily under your arm or you may accompany bags weighing up to 70 lbs. each. (Such bags travel in the baggage compartment of the aircraft.) But generally, the only thing you carry will be the document pouch that usually weighs less than five pounds. It must be kept with you at all times.

You'll *not* be transporting or accompanying anything illegal. Courier companies have long-standing reputations to protect. All shipments are inspected by bonded personnel prior to being manifested. Therefore, it is safe to assume you will not be engaged to transport illicit goods.

In addition, custom officers know that couriers never touch the shipment they accompany.

Personal Luggage

Generally, a courier's personal luggage is limited to a single carry-on bag. That is not a problem for most seasoned travelers who believe that less is more, anyway. Also, having all your belongings in your possession can save you a considerable amount of time when clearing customs.

If you feel you need more than just a carry-on, it may be permissable for you to bring a backpack, a tote, and a purse or camera case. But as there is no standardized airline industry policy regarding carry-on baggage allowances, be sure to call for specifics prior to your flight.

If you insist on multiple carry-ons and/or checking additional bags, we have a few suggestions for you:

1. Ask the courier company for specifics concerning your baggage allowance on this particular flight. The company may not need its usual amount of baggage space.
2. Ask the reservation agent at the ticket counter if you can check an extra at no cost. Agents sometimes honor such requests.
3. Pay an "excess baggage" fee at the check-in desk. (Call ahead for prices—and be sure to check with the courier company to be sure there is no conflict.)

Because of luggage size restrictions, you will want to pack well. Coordinate your clothes and limit the number of outfits. Bring wash-and-wear clothes that can be laundered in your hotel bathroom. Take along the small, sample sizes of toiletries available in most drugstores. Remember that most courier flights are not to the wilds of Africa—you *will* be able to purchase almost anything you might leave behind.

Air Courier Requirements and Qualifications
Most courier companies require that you be at least 21 years old. You must also have a valid passport.

Most companies also require a driver's license and major credit card for the purpose of identification.

If you are flying into a country that requires a visa, you must obtain one prior to departure.

You must be in good health and strong enough to do light lifting. (Occasionally, couriers must load bags onto a baggage cart in the customs hall.)

Generally speaking, one's nationality does not matter.

Rules and Responsibilities

There are some important terms to which a courier must agree. For instance:

- The courier is generally expected to "report for duty" one day prior to the scheduled return flight.
- The courier is expected to keep his security/manifest papers in his sight at all times.
- The courier's baggage allowance is often limited to carry-on items only; no check-in items. This can vary, however, so be sure to discuss the matter during your first contact call.

Failure to Follow Through

If you fail to complete your assignment in every respect, you will have denied yourself the opportunity of ever flying so cheaply again with that courier company, and probably many others because they network. You may also lose your security deposit and even your return ticket.

Dress Code

Dress standards reflect the company's image, so you are expected to dress accordingly. Both casual clothing and business attire are acceptable to most companies. However, shorts, thongs, suggestive T-shirts and "unconventional" hair styles are not tolerated. Blue jeans are allowed by some courier companies providing they are clean, without holes and unfaded.

Some companies specify that their air couriers are not permitted to drink alcohol before or during the flight.

In summary, couriers must look and act like someone a customs official would not hesitate to admit to his country.

Departure Taxes

Couriers are responsible for paying departure taxes. Check with your country of destination to learn how much that will be.

Clearing Customs

The procedure for clearing customs varies from country to country. Specific regulations will be found on the information sheet given you by the courier company at the beginning of your trip.

In some countries, a company representative will meet you and clear the documents; in other countries you will need to clear the documents yourself.

The Pricing of Courier Tickets

Courier companies purchase their tickets from the airlines and prices depend upon the agreement between the two of them. Call various courier services to find out what is available at any given time.

> *Note: you are not buying an airline ticket, you are buying a courier trip; the courier company purchased the ticket and it belongs to them. Your name may or may not be on the ticket. (If your name does appear on the ticket, be sure to ask that the flight mileage be credited to your frequent flyer account.)*

Deposit Required

Interestingly enough, courier companies learned early on that if they charged couriers no money at all, many failed to show up for their assigned flight! Thus the origin of the shared ticket concept.

Accordingly, they will want either a deposit or full payment for your portion of the airline ticket well in advance of departure. The deposit, approximately $500, will be returned to you after you have successfully completed the duties outlined in your courier contract.

You can usually pay with a money order, certified check or sometimes, a personal check. Some courier companies will take a credit card as well.

Receiving Your Air Courier Ticket

Courier companies use various procedures for giving a courier his plane ticket. Often, couriers are instructed to meet a company representative at the airport terminal.

Sometimes, couriers are instead asked to report to the company's office, usually located near the airport; the company will then ferry the courier to the airport. In such cases, the driver will often assist with the check-in of the cargo.

Note: You must be punctual. Car trouble, heavy traffic, late connecting flights, etc. are not acceptable excuses for lateness at either end of your trip.

Remaining at Your Destination

Courier trips vary in length. Some companies have predetermined return dates that cannot be altered while other companies allow stays lasting from days to months.

Note: If the company says you must return on "x" date, they mean "x" date—no negotiations! Be careful about pushing them too hard—there are a lot of other couriers available out there!

Your Return Ticket

In some cases, you will receive return flight instructions along with your return ticket at the time of departure. Other times, you will be asked to meet with a company representative at your destination city in order to obtain your return ticket.

Most courier companies require that you be in your departure city 24 hours prior to the actual departure time. That is important for you as well, as flight schedules often change.

And of course, in order to return to the U.S., you must have your re-entry papers.

Planning a Trip as a Courier

There are three common ways to plan for a trip as a courier. You can:

1. select a destination with approximate departure and return dates, then call the courier companies to see if they are interested in using your services
2. select a destination, call an air courier service, and take whatever dates available
3. select your travel dates and take whatever *destination* is available

Departure Cities

Air courier flights generally depart from New York, Los Angeles, Miami, Chicago, Dallas, San Francisco, Toronto, Montreal and Vancouver.

Destination Cities

The most common destinations at the present time are Australia, England, France, Germany, Guatemala, Hong Kong, Japan, Korea, New Zealand, Peru, Singapore Taiwan, Thailand and Venezuela.

Generally, New York services Europe, Miami services Latin America and California services Asia and Australia.

Domestic Courier Flights

For the most part, the. domestic market for free lance air couriers has diminished considerably in recent years.

Advance Planning

You can begin planning early because most courier companies book flights as much as two months in advance.

On the other hand, last minute changes do occur and you can sometimes get an even greater deal just prior to a flight's departure. And the closer the deadline, the better the deal!

If you want to book for a heavily traveled time of year, find out what day the "books" open and call in on that day to make a reservation. If you book far enough in advance, you may get the exact flight of your choice.

Vacation Planning

You will be able to make vacation plans around courier schedules most of the time. If the courier company changes your flight schedule at all, it will generally be to the day before or the day after the original date.

If your flight is delayed or canceled by the airline, you are entitled to the same treatment and/or compensation as any other passenger with respect to cancellations and delays.

Arranging to Travel With a Friend

Courier companies generally only need one courier for a destination at a given time,. However, they can sometimes schedule additional couriers to the same destination, but on consecutive days.

It is also possible for two people to go to the same destination on the same day, but for different courier companies and on different airlines. Do your research.

Either way, it is recommended that you use a courier booking *agency* for your convenience when you want to travel with another person since such firms have access to multiple courier company schedules.

The most common way for two people to travel as couriers to the same destination is to arrange to have your companion booked on a later flight—perhaps even the next day.

Another way is for one person to book as a courier while the companion pays for a regular ticket (or a consolidator ticket). As a couple, you still will have saved a lot of money!

Ticket Upgrades

You cannot upgrade a courier flight. You must be willing to fly in economy class. However, if the flight isn't full, you may be able to move to a better seat in the same class of service.

Frequent Flyer Mileage Credits

Some airlines allow couriers to earn frequent flyer mileage; others do not. It always pays to ask. When you check in, tell the reservation agent you want your flight credited to your frequent flyer account. Then give the agent your airline ticket/stub, say nothing else—and wait for a response.

Ask If a Better Deal is Available

Ask if there are any last minute specials. Typically, courier companies offer last minute fares only to those people who have flown with them before.

Hotel Accommodations

Courier companies are not travel agents, so don't expect them to make other arrangements for you.

On the other hand, travel agencies specializing in courier flights *can* make other travel arrangements for you (connecting flights, hotels, etc.)

Shipping Things Home

If you plan to shop internationally, don't ship your purchases home to yourself; customs only allows you to ship $25 per-day-per-address. Instead, if you need extra space, ship your clothing to yourself and carry your purchases in your suitcase!

"Duty Free" Allowance

All passengers, including couriers, are allowed to bring $400 of duty free purchases into the United States providing they are in compliance with U.S. Customs regulations. The next $1,000 is charged a flat 10%.

Courier Travel Agents

Rather than scouring courier companies one by one, you might consider using a courier booking agency. The main courier booking agencies are located in New York.

The advantages to using an agency's services are: (a) you get a broader range of destinations; (b) they often have last-minute flights which are substantially cheaper; (c) sometimes they have free flights. A courier travel agency can also book connecting flights, arrange hotels and car rentals and meet other travel needs.

Another big advantage is that an agency is more likely to arrange for two people to fly on the same flight because they book for multiple courier companies.

The disadvantages of not going through a courier company and using a courier travel agency instead include: (a) having to pay a fee for the agency's services; (b) some agencies also charge a membership fee.

Only if you are planning to take a lot flights, should you join a courier membership program in advance. And always join at the last possible moment, because your membership is only good for one year from the date of purchase.

When calling a courier company directly, tell them you are a free lance air courier and you would like to book a flight. All you have to do is say where you want to go—and pay your money.

Courier Organizations

There are two organizations that keep budget-minded travelers updated on courier flights and other budget-travel options: *International Association of Air Travel Couriers* (IAATC) and the *Air Courier Association* (ACA).

IAATC charges $45 annually per household. They may be reached at 561/582-8320. Their Internet address is: http://www.courier.org.

ACA charges a $64 first-year membership fee and $39 for successive years. They may be reached at 303/279-3600. Their Internet address is: http://www.aircourier.org.

Important Questions to Ask a Courier Company

When you call a courier company, it is important that you ask the following questions:

• Will I fly as an air courier *both* ways?
• What is the minimum and maximum length of stay allowed by your company?

- May I check my luggage or will I be limited to carry-on baggage only?
- Is a visa required?
- What is your company's booking procedure?
- Are there any other restrictions I should know about?

Courier Company Directory

There are other books available that are devoted to flying as a free lance courier. But *Airfare Secrets Exposed* has the most comprehensive listing of VALID courier companies anywhere!

You should be aware of the fact that courier flights and destinations change rapidly. So if you are serious about flying as an air courier, join **The International Association of Air Travel Couriers** for their updated newsletters, fax-on-demand-service and on-line courier flight availability. Here are some of the other benefits they offer:

- information is updated daily
- up to date fare information
- a listing of which airlines fly to which destinations
- the name of the person to contact at the courier company
- a detailed listing of minimum and maximum length of stays

The most common destinations for courier companies have been included here to aid you in deciding which courier company or courier travel agency to call first.

Because prices, airlines flown, and length of stays change constantly, we chose not to include that information here.

DOMESTIC

Boston

Air Cargo Partners
1983 Marcus Avenue 3108
Lake Success, NY 11042

Tel: 516/358-2025
Fax: 516/358-1835

From Boston to:
        London
        --connecting flights to various other cities

Chicago

Rapid Air Systems
967 Graceland Avenue #9
Des Plaines, Il 60016

Tel: 847/375-8580
Fax: 847/375-8582

From Chicago to:
        London
        Brussels

Guam

DHL Worldwide
P.O. Box 7269
Tamuning, Guam 96931

Tel: 671/646-6753
Fax: 671/646-9354

From Guam to:
Honolulu

| Los   Angeles |

East West Express
P.O. Box 300849
JFK Airport Station
Jamaica, NY 11430

Tel: 718/656-6246
Fax: 718/656-6247

From Los Angeles to:
Auckland
New Zealand
Brisbane
Cairns
Melbourne
Sydney

International Bonded Couriers (IBC Pacific)
5793 W. Imperial Highway
Los Angeles International Airport
Los Angeles, CA 90045.

Tel: 310/665-1760
Fax: 310/665-0247

From Los Angeles to:
Bangkok
Hong Kong
Manila
Seoul
Thailand

Jupiter Air
460 S. Hindry Avenue, Unit D
Inglewood, CA 90301

Tel: 310/670-1197
Fax: 310/670-1198

From Los Angeles to:
    Seoul
    Bangkok
    Hong Kong

Air Cargo Partners
1983 Marcus Avenue 3108
Lake Success, NY 11042

Tel: 516/358-2025
Fax: 516/358-1835

From Los Angeles to:
    London
    --connecting flights to various other cities

Miami

Trans Air Systems
7264 NW 25th Street
Miami, FL 33122

Tel: 305/592-1771
Fax: 305/592-2927

From Miami to:
    Guatemala City
    Quito

Lima Service
6115 Johnson Street
Hollywood, FL 33024

Tel: 954/964-8400
Fax: 954/964-0700

From Miami to:
   Lima

Air Cargo Partners
1983 Marcus Avenue #108
Lake Success, NY 11042

Tel: 516/358-2025
Fax: 516/358-1835

From Miami to:
   London
   --connecting flights to various other cities

International Bonded Couriers (IBC)
8401 NW 17th Street
Miami, FL 33126

Tel: 305/597-5331
Fax: 305/591-2056

From Miami to:
   Buenos Aires
   Santiago

Air Facility
7227 NW 32nd Street
Miami, FL 33122

Tel: 305/418-2035
Fax: 305/418-2055
From Miami to:
   Buenos Aires
   Sao Paulo
   Rio de Janeiro

New York

Micom America (Jupiter Air)
Building #14, JFK Int. Airport
Jamaica, NY 11430

Tel: 718/656-6050
Fax: 718/656-7263

From New York to:
    Hong Kong
    London

Global Delivery Systems
147-05 176th Street
Jamaica, NY 11434

Tel: 718/995-7300
Fax: 718/995-9067

From New York to:
    Brussels
    Amsterdam
    Rome
    Milan
    Madrid
    London
    Paris
    Copenhagen
    Dublin
    Tokyo
    Singapore
    Hong Kong
    Bangkok
    Manila

World Courier, Inc.
1313 4th Avenue
New Hyde Park, NY 11040

Tel: 516/354-2600
Fax: 516/354-2637

From New York to:
    Mexico City

Air Cargo Partners
1983 Marcus Avenue #108
Lake Success, NY 11042

Tel: 516/358-2024
Fax: 516/358-1835

From New York to:
    London
    --connecting flights to various other cities

Air Facility
153-40 Rockaway Blvd.
Jamaica, NY 11434

Tel: 718/712-1769
Fax: 718/712-1574

From New York to:
    Buenos Aires
    Rio de Janeiro
    Montevideo
    Sao Paulo
    Caracas

Now Voyager
74 Varick Street, Suite 307
New York, NY 11013

Tel 212/431-1616
Fax: 212/334-5234

From New York to:
    London
    Dublin

Milan
Rome
Madrid
Paris
Brussels
Amsterdam
Copenhagen
Buenos Aires
Rio de Janeiro
Sao Paulo
Caracas
Hong Kong
Tokyo
Singapore
Bangkok
Beijing
Taipei
Manila
Seoul
Johannesburg

Courier Network
515 W. 29th Street
New York, NY 10001

Tel: 212/947-3738
Fax: 212/947-2352

From New York to:
    Tel Aviv

East West Express
P.O. Box 300849
JFK Airport Station
Jamaica, NY 11430

Tel: 718/656-6246
Fax: 718/656-6247

From New York to:
    Johannesburg

Capetown
Sydney
Melbourne
Brisbane
Cairns
Auckland
Shanghai
Beijing
Taipei
Bangkok
Hong Kong
Tokyo
Seoul
Manila
Kuala Lumpur

As You Like It Travel
224 West 35th Street, Suite 1126
New York, NY 10001

Tel: 212/216-0644
Fax: 212/947-6117

From New York to:
Brussels
Dublin
Madrid
London
Paris
Hong Kong

Newark

Air Cargo Partners
1983 Marcus Avenue #108
Lake Success, NY 11042

Tel: 516/358-2025
Fax 516/358-1835

From Newark to:
    London
    --connecting flights to various other cities

| **San Francisco** |

Jupiter Air
839 Hinckley Road, Suite A
Burlingame, CA 94010
Tel: 650/697-1773
Fax: 650/697-7892

From San Francisco to:
    Singapore
    Manila

Air Cargo Partners
1983 Marcus Avenue #108
Lake Success, NY 11042

Tel: 516/358-2025
Fax 516/358-1835

From San Francisco to:
    London
    --connecting flights to various other cities

UTL Travel
320 Corey Way
South San Francisco, CA 94080

Tel: 650/583-5074
Fax: 650/583-8122

From San Francisco to:
    Singapore
    Manila

Washington DC

Air Cargo Partners
1983 Marcus Avenue #108
Lake Success, NY 11042

Tel: 516/358-1835
Fax: 516/358-1835

From Washington, DC to:
London
--connecting flights to various other cities

FOREIGN

Argentina

Air Facility
P.O. Box 224
Mascot, NSW 2020
Australia

Tel: 011-54-114-362-1016

From Buenos Aires to:
Sao Paulo
Rio de Janeiro
Montevideo

Austrailia

Jupiter Air
P.O. Box 224
Mascot, NSW 2020
Australia

Tel: 011-61-29-317-2230
Fax: 011-61-29-317-2238
Courier Contact: Robert

From Sydney to:
        London

Canada

FB On Board Courier Service
5110 Fairway Street, Lachine
Quebec H8T 1B8

Tel: 514/631-2677

From Vancouver to:
        London

England

British Airways Travel Shops
Room E328-332, 3rd Floor E Block
BA Craneback S554 Off Jubilee Way
Hounslow, Middlesex TW6 2JA
United Kingdom

Tel: 011-44-870-606-1133
Fax: 011-44-181-562-3066

From London to:
        Budapest
        New York
        Newark
        Boston
        Chicago
        Miami
        Philadelphia
        San Francisco

Washington, DC
Seattle
Mexico City
Buenos Aires
Mauritius Islands
Bangkok
Tokyo

Nomad Courier Service
664 Hanworth Road
Hounslow,
Middlesex TW4 5NP
England

Tel: 011-44-181-893-3820
Fax: 011-44-181-898-2117

From London to:
New York

British Airways Travel Shops
P.O. Box 10
Heathrow Airport
Hounslow, Middlesex TW6 2JA
United Kingdom

Tel: 011-44-870-606-1133
Fax: 011-44-181-562-3066

From London to:
Budapest
New York
Newark
Boston
Chicago
Miami
Philadelphia
San Francisco
Washington DC
Seattle
Mexico City

Buenos Aires
Mauritius islands
Bangkok
Tokyo

Air Cargo Partners
Travel Dept.
Unit 8, Radius Park
Middlesex TW14 ONG
England

Tel: 011-181-44-897-5130
Fax: 011-44-181-897-5133

From: London to:
New York
Newark
Boston
Orlando
Los Angeles
San Francisco
Washington, DC
Sydney
Melbourne
Johannesburg
Tokyo
Hong Kong

Ecuador

Trans Air Systems
7264 NW 25th Street
Miami, FL 33122

Tel: 305/592-1771
Fax: 305/592-2927

From Quito to:
Miami

France

Halbart Express
39-39 Rue Broca
5th Arrondissement
Paris, France

Tel: 011-33-1-45-87-32-30

From Paris to:
New York

Guatemala

Trans Air Systems
7264 NW 25th Street
Miami, FL 33122

Tel: 305/592-1771
Fax: 305/592-2927

From Guatemala to:
Miami

Hong Kong

Jupiter Air Ltd.
Room 1701, Tower #1
China Hong Kong City
33 Canton Road
Tsimshatshi, Kowloon
Hong Kong

Tel: 011-852-2735-1946/47
Fax: 011-852-2735-0450

From Hong Kong to:

New York
Tokyo

Linehaul Express (Cathay Pacific)
11/F-14/F Lao Seng Comm. Centre
4-6 Hankow Road
Kowloon, Hong Kong

Tel: 011-852-2316-1997
Fax: 011-852-2311-2639

From Hong Kong to:
    Bangkok
    Tokyo
    Taipei
    Seoul
    Shanghai

Dyna Trans (Hong Kong) Ltd.
5th Floor, 152 Queen's Road Central
Hong Kong

Tel: 011-852-2851-6120
Fax: 011-852-2545-3331

From Hong Kong to:
    London
    Manila

Bridges Worldwide
Room 908, Pacific Trade Center
2 Kai Hing Road
Kowloon Bay
Hong Kong

Tel: 011-852-2305-1412
Fax: 011-852-2795-8312

From Hong Kong to:
    Sydney
    Bangkok

Aeronet Express Hong Kong Ltd.
Rm. 203 Good Harvest Air Freight Centre
70-78 Sung Wong Toi Road to Kwa Wan Kowloon
Hong Kong

Tel: 011-852-2751-6186
Fax: 011-852-2755-8467

From Hong Kong to:
    Jakarta
    Kuala Lumpur
    London
    Singapore

Japan

Fastlink Express
Hello Bldg. 302 575-224 Nanae
Tomisato-macni
Inba-gun
Chiba 286-02221

Tel: 011-81-4-7691-2895
Fax: 011-81-4-7691-0313

From Tokyo to:
    Bangkok
    Hong Kong
    Singapore

South Korea

Jupiter Express
P.O. Box 8705
Seoul, Korea 682-3
Kong Hang Tong, Kang Suang Ku
Seoul, South Korea

Tel: 011-82-2-665-6024
Fax: 011-82-2-665-1777

From Seoul to:
    Los Angeles
    New York

New Zealand

TNT Express Worldwide
6 Doncaster Street, Mangere
Auckland, New Zealand

Tel: 011-64-9-255-0549
Fax: 011-64-9-255-0501

From Auckland to:
    Los Angeles
    San Francisco
    Frankfurt
    Honolulu
    Seattle
    Vancouver

Singapore

Air United
107A Killiney Road
Singapore, 239547

Tel: 011-65-735-7684
Fax: 011-65-735-7584

From Singapore to:
    San Francisco
    Manila

Airtropolis   Express
SATS Express & Courier Centre
Unit #01-04 Singapore Changi Airport
Singapore 819459

Tel: 011-65-545-3686
Fax: 011-65-545-2055

From Singapore to:
      Bangkok
      Kuala Lumpur

Thailand

Siam Trans International
78 Kiatnakin Bldg.
Bushland, New Road
Bangkok 10500, Thailand

Tel: 011-66-2-237-3061
Fax: 011-66-2-236-1042

From Bangkok to:
      Hong Kong
      Los Angeles
      San Francisco

OBC Courier
Vanit Bldg. #1, 16th Fl., Rm. 1605
1126/1 New Petchburi Rd.
Bangkok 10400

Tel: 011-66-2-255-8590
Fax: 011-66-2-255-8593

From Bangkok to:
      Singapore

4

AIR PASSES—BARGAIN PRICES "OVER THERE"

An air pass is actually a "multi-flight coupon book" of discount tickets offered by an airline to travelers who reside in a different country. They may not be called, air passes per se (*Intra-Europe Flights* is another name, for instance), but they all are essentially the same.

The air pass is the airlines' answer to the popular Eurail-pass. If you plan to explore a country thoroughly and don't particularly like long bus or train rides, the air pass is a good means for getting about quickly and more economically than buying tickets one at a time.

Generally, you must purchase your air pass *before* arriving in your destination city. *Often, air passes must be purchased from the same airline you will use for the international portion of your journey.* Some airlines will still sell you an air pass even if you do not fly internationally with them—but at a higher rate.

The easiest way to obtain information regarding air pass availability is to contact a knowledgeable travel agent and ask for information regarding air pass programs available for the countries you intend to visit.

However, you can also book most air passes on your own. Be aware of the fact that *you will need to specify your various destination cities ahead of time for most air pass programs*, even though some passes allow you frequent flights once there.

Also, you will have to specify the starting and ending dates for your air pass at the time of purchase, even though the intermediate flight dates can usually be left open.

Intra-Europe Flight Program

At the time of the writing of this book, fourteen airlines are participants in a program called *Europe by Air* that has a uniform policy regarding intra-European flights. You can reach *Europe by Air* by telephone at 888/387-2479 or on the Internet: http://www.europebyair.com.

Participating airlines charge $99 per flight with a purchase of three non-transferable, non-refundable coupons that are valid for 120 days and can only be purchased in North America. You can get this bargain regardless of which airline you used for your flight to Europe.

Participating airlines are:

> Air Greece
> Air Liberte
> Air One
> Alpi Eagles
> Augsburg Airways
> CityJet
> Croatia Airlines
> Debonair
> Estonian Air

Icelandair
Portugalia
Spanair
TTA
Virgin Express
VLM

Here is a comprehensive directory of all airlines with air passes available and the name of their passes.

Remember, not all airlines call them air passes, so be sure to *describe the type of intra-Europe ticket you are seeking* if the agent doesn't immediately respond to "air pass."

Aero Peru
Visit South America: 800/777-7717

Aerolineas Argentinas
Visit Argentina: 800/333-0276

Air France
Euroflyer Pass: 800/237-2747

Air India
Discover India: 800/223-7776

Air New Zealand
Air Pass: 800/262-1234

Antiquitie Tours
Air Pass: 800/354-7471

Avianca
Discover Colombia: 800/284-2622

Aviateca
Mayan Pass Fares: 800/327-9832

British Airways
Air Pass: 800/247-9297

Canadian Airlines International
Visit USA Fares: 800/426-7000

Faucett, The First Airline of Peru
Visit Peru: 800/334-3356

Finnair
Holiday Pass: 800/950-5000

Garuda Indonesian Airways
Visit Indonesia - Air Tickets: 800/342-7832

Hawaiian Airlines
Hawaiian Air Pass: 800/367-5320

Iberia Airlines of Spain
Visit Spain: 800/772-4642

Ladeco Airlines
Visit Chile: 800/825-2332

Lan-Chile Airlines
Visit Chile: 800/735-5526

Lloyd Aereo Boliviano Airlines
Visit Bolivia: 800/327-7407

Malaysia Airlines
Discover Malaysia Pass: 800/552-9264

Mexicana
Air Pass: 800/531-7921

Qantas Airlines
Australia Explorer Pass: 800/227-4500

Royal Air Moroc
Discover Morocco: 800/344-6726

Scandinavian Airlines
Visit Scandinavia: 800/221-2350

South African Airways
Africa Explorer: 800/722-9675

Thai Airways International
Discover Thailand: 800/426-5204

Trans Brazil
Visit Brazil: 800/872-3153

Varig Brasilian Airlines
Brasil Pass: 800/468-2744

5

STATUS FARES—
SAVINGS FOR BEING
"SOMEONE SPECIAL"

Status Fares

Status fares are those that relate to who you are rather than how you want to travel or where you want to go. Status fares most often fall under such headings as: Senior, Student, Compassionate/Bereavement, Children, Youth, Clergy, and Family—and more (see below).

The authors conducted an informal survey of eight domestic airlines to determine just how available such discount fares are at the present time. Printed below are the results of that survey. Keep in mind that airline policies and fare availability's change frequently.

Status Fare Savings

Not all airlines honor all status fares discussed in this chapter. Of those that do, you can generally expect the following accommodations:

- Senior: 10% discount
- Youth/Student: Published discounts on selected routes
- Child: Varies by route
- Infant: Children under two years of age may fly at half-fare discount on most airlines (or free if on an adult's lap)
- Compassionate/bereavement: 50%-70% off. (funerals always count; severe family illness counts with selected airlines)

Student Discount:
Yes:	1
No:	4
Limited markets:	1
International:	2

Compassionate/Bereavement Fare Discount:
Yes:	8
No:	0

Children's Discount:
Yes:	1
No:	4
Limited markets:	3

Family Discount:
Yes:	0
No:	5
Limited markets:	3

Senior Discount:

Yes:	8
No:	0

Clergy Discount:

Yes:	2
No:	6

Group Discount:

Yes:	8
No:	0

7-day Advance Purchase Discount:

Yes:	8
No:	0

14-day Advance Purchase Discount:

Yes:	8
No:	0

21-day Advance Purchase Discount:

Yes:	2
No:	2
Selected markets:	4

30-day Advance Purchase Discount:

Yes:	1
No:	7

Off-Peak Discount:

Yes:	2
No:	3
Limited markets:	3

Prove It!

You must be prepared to prove your eligibility for a status fare, both when you buy your ticket and again when you travel. Proof of age is required for senior, children, and youth fares; a school ID for student fares, and a funeral or death notice (or the equivalent) for a bereavement/compassionate fare.

Status fares are published, so you can buy your ticket directly from the airline or through a travel agency.

Senior Coupons—a Real Bargain!

Approximately eight US airlines presently sell booklets containing four senior coupons, each one good for a one-way coach trip within the 48 contiguous states.

The coupon book costs about $600, meaning that a senior can take a round-trip for about $300—about half the usual year-round fare.

Note: the coupons are valid for a year, meaning that you must take at least two round-trips in that period to maximize your savings.

Senior Clubs

Delta, American and United airlines have formed Senior Clubs which offer zone-based fares that range from approximately $100 to $575 round-trip for travel within the 48 contiguous states. One-way fares are half of the round-trip plus $10.

There are a few qualifications and restrictions, but Senior Clubs still offer excellent savings to those who qualify.

6

BUDGET TRAVEL
VIA THE INTERNET

An informed industry source says that 6.7 million people used the Internet to make airline reservations in 1998, up from 5.4 million in 1997.

There is a good reason for such interest. Savvy Internet shoppers can go on-line and, searching multiple web sites, come up with prices that airlines and travel agents oftentimes can't match. And if they wish, they can fare-shop twenty-four hours a day.

The savings can be substantial. For instance, *Priceline.com* claims that their customers save an average of 43%. Rules and procedures vary from company to company, so make sure you understand all conditions before you click the "purchase" button.

There are hundreds of web sites for airline fare bargain-seekers. The trouble isn't in finding them, but instead in determining which are most credible and productive.

Following, the authors list some of their favorites:

Airfare.com
http://www.air-fare.com
This site lists in ranking order, the lowest fares for forty top U.S. cities.

Air-Tech
http://www.airtech.com
This site offers great savings to those willing and able to travel on a short notice of two- to four-days.

AuctionWatch
http://www.auctionwatch.com
This site tracks fare auctions.

Bidder's Edge
http://www.biddersedge.com
This site tracks fare auctions.

Expedia Travel News
http://expedia.msn.com
This site features a daily Bargain Watch. Their Travel Wise section offers insightful advice.

Frommer's
http://www.frommers.com

Budget travel advice. Excellent country-by-country books that can save you bundles.

IntelliTRIP.com
http://intellitrip.com
This is a program that combs through multiple airline web sites to find the best price—including unpublished fares.

Internet Travel Network
http://www.itn.net
This site operates in a unique manner: Tell them your destination and price ceiling, and they'll alert you by e-mail when a matching flight is available.

Lowest-fare.com
http://www.lowestfare.com
This site tracks web specials.

Luxury Link
http://www.luxurylink.com
This site tracks fare auctions.

Preview Travel
http://www.previewtravel.com
This site's *Farefinder* makes it easy to find the most affordable flights to cities around the world.

Priceline.Com
http://www.priceline.com
This site boasts an intriguing concept: you tell them how much you would like to pay for your next flight, and see if an airline will accept your offer,

SkyAuction
http://www.skyauction.com
This site tracks fare auctions.

Smarter Living
http://www.smarterliving.com
This site tracks web specials.

Travelbreak.com
http://www.travelbreak.com
This site, launched October of 1999, promises to deliver bargains via travel auctions, fixed-price deals, and travel-related products

Travelocity Travel News
http://www.travelocity.com/news/newfares.html
This site offers rapid access to dozens of fare options.

Travel Discounts
http://www.traveldiscounts.com
This site offers 1.5 million discounted airfares and hotel accommodations

Tom Parsons' Best Fares
http://www.bestfares.com
This site lists low-cost deals on flights, hotels and car rentals.

Webflyer
http://www.webflyer.com
This site helps travelers maximize their frequent flyer miles by disclosing special offers, mileage bonuses, and other insider information.

Worldwide Courier Association
http://www.massiveweb.com
This site offers incredibly low fares, mostly to overseas destinations, for those willing to travel as couriers (which translates to no luggage). Membership fee required.

Yahoo Travel
http://travel.yahoo.com/
This site offers rapid access to dozens of fare options.

1Travel.Com
http://www.onetravel.com
This site lists everything from discount airfares and hotel rates to cruise deals. They will even send you weekly e-mails alerting you to last minute bargains.

The Airlines' Own Sites

Informed sources say that 31% of consumers visiting airline sites are booking vs. 21% in 1998. That 68% increase in a single year says that people must like doing business this way.

Alaska Airlines
http://www.alaskaair.com
This site posts web specials on Tuesdays for last-minute weekend travel plus specials for travel any time.

American
http://www.aa.com
This site posts New SAAver Fares on Wednesdays for travel two weekends later. The site also permits users to price and book flights on other airlines.

Continental
http://www.continental.com
This site posts travel specials on Tuesday for Saturday departures that return Mondays or Tuesdays.

Delta
http://www.delta-air.com
This site posts special fares on Wednesdays.

Northwest
http://www.nwa.com
This site posts special fares on Wednesdays.

Southwest
http://www.iflyswa.com
This site posts special fares on Tuesdays. You can stay informed by signing up for e-mail postings.

TWA
http://www.twa.com
This site posts special fares on Wednesdays for Friday or Saturday departures returning on Mondays or Tuesdays.

United
http://www.ual.com
This site posts special fares on Wednesday for departures on Saturday, returning Sunday to Tuesday. International fares (not necessarily with weekend departures), are posted Thursdays. Site also permits users to price and book flights on other airlines.

US Airways
http://usairways.com
This site posts special fares Thursday mornings for Saturday departures that return Sunday to Tuesday.

7

CHARTER AIRLINES
OFFER SAVINGS

Charter flights are those on which large groups of seats are purchased for the purpose of being marketed to a particular group of travelers. For instance, a student charter business might offer a flight to Europe exclusively for card-carrying students, while another flight might be set aside for ferrying a planeload of people from cold, northern cities to a warm, tropical destination.

Charters fares are often lower than regular excursion fares. But one should compare prices carefully because sale prices by major airlines as well as regular prices from low-fare airlines and consolidator fares sometimes undercut charter prices.

The downside to charter flights is that they do not depart as frequently as other types of flights—and they often sell out quickly.

It is also worth noting that charter flights are not very flexible with regard to cancellations or departure/return dates.

Charter Directory

Charters can be located and booked through your travel agent as some wholesale tour operators sell only through retail travel agencies.

You can also buy directly from some of the charter companies but your flight will probably not be any cheaper and it's likely you'll receive less personal service.

The authors have listed in alphabetical order below, a number of established charter lines.

AirHitch   800/326-2009
   http://www.airhitch.org

AirTech   800/575-8324
   http://www.airtech.com

Corsair   800/677-0720
   http://www.corsair-int.com

Jet Express   888/806-8823
   http://www.jetexpress.com

Martinair   800/627-8462
   http://www.martinair.com

Myrtle Beach Jet Express   800/386-2786
   http://www.myrtlebeachjetexp.com

SunJet   800/478-6538
   http://www.sunjet.com

8

GOOD TIMING =
BIG $AVING$!

Airlines Own and Control the Fare System

ATPCO (Airline Tariff Publishing Company) is the organization that collects and distributes airline fare information. ATPCO (sometimes referred to as "fare central" by insiders, is a for-profit corporation located near Washington Dulles International Airport.

ATPCO collects fare information from over 550 airlines and then distributes it via various global distribution systems, thereby enabling airlines to both see almost instantaneously what others are charging—and then to post their own fares.

APTCO is owned by the following airlines:
Air Canada
Air France

Alaska Airlines, Inc.
Aloha Airlines, Inc.
American Airlines, Inc.
British Airways
Canadian Airlines International, Ltd.
Chicago Helicopter Airways, Inc.
Continental Airlines, Inc.
Delta Air Lines, Inc.
Federal Express Corp.
Hawaiian Airlines, Inc.
Iberia Air Lines of Spain
Japan Airlines
KLM Royal Dutch Airlines
LA Helicopter, Inc.
Lufthansa German Airlines
Northwest Airlines, Inc.
Reeve Aleutian Airways, Inc.
Scandinavian Airlines System
Swissair
Trans World Airlines, Inc.
United Air Lines, Inc.
US Airways, Inc.

Fares Can Change Three Times a Day!

To change fares, its participating airlines worldwide must send their adjustments via telecommunication or fax to the ATPCO system. Next, ATPCO informs its paying subscribers, who in turn inform the rest of the world.

Airlines can change airfares up to three times each weekday, at 10 A.M., 12:30 P.M. and 8 P.M., Eastern Standard Time. On Saturdays and Sundays, they may only enter fare changes at 5 P.M.

Note: International flight prices can be changed four times daily—but that's a story for another time.

Since most airlines open flight bookings about 325 days before departure, it is theoretically possible that the selling price for each seat could change more than 800 times before takeoff!

Dozens of Fares on Each Flight

Neither ATPCO nor the federal government places a limit on the number of fares that can be offered on a single flight. Therefore, it is entirely possible that passengers seated within the same cabin will have paid dozens of different prices.

Unrestricted tickets—the costliest seats—are typically sold to business travelers who want the privilege of being able to alter their flight schedule. Such tickets do not require a Saturday night stay-over.

Cheaper tickets are sold to those who buy in advance and to those who have a Saturday night stay-over. This rule came into play to separate budget-minded tourists from deep-pocketed business travelers.

Bargain Seats are Limited

Airlines do everything they can to attract the attention of potential buyers. They'll announce a reduced fare, for instance, from city A to city B, selling tickets at $100 instead of the usual $175. What they're not saying is *how many* of those $100 bargain seats are actually available. They might mark down 30, 20 or even just 10 seats in an attempt to lure buyers—and they're not obliged to disclose how many exist.

According to federal law, however, once a price is advertised, at least 10% of the tickets in that segment of the market must be sold at that price. Airline insiders refer to these price categories as "buckets." And on a Boeing 737, which carries about 100 coach passengers, it's common for an airline to offer seven "bucket seats" on sale at one time.

Check Fares After Noon on Friday

Some airline industry insiders say fare changes are most often announced on Friday afternoons so that the airline can see how it works through the weekend, when sales volume is lower and the price change is less risky for the airline. Then on Monday, they can decide whether to hold that price or retreat to the higher fare.

Airlines Discount On Their Own Web Sites

Airlines themselves, ever eager to bypass travel agent commissions, now announce special discounts on their web sites. The authors have included airline web site addresses in Appendix 8. You might want to become familiar with their those addresses so you can become a more astute ticket shopper.

As recently as just a year or two ago, an airline's web site was the *last* place you would check if you were seeking bargain fares.

It just goes to show you how fast things change!

9

GET BUMPED—
GET CA$H!

Overbooking is not illegal and most airlines overbook their scheduled flights to a certain degree in order to compensate for no-shows. Passengers are sometimes left behind or "bumped" as a result. When an oversell occurs, the Department of Transportation (DOT) requires that airlines ask people who are not in a hurry to give up their seats voluntarily in exchange for compensation.

Passengers who are bumped against their will are *entitled to compensation.*

Voluntary Bumping

At the check-in or boarding area of an over-booked flight, check-in attendants will make an announcement seeking passengers who are willing to be bumped. If it is not important that you arrive at your destination at the time originally planned, you may wish to forfeit your reservation to the airline in exchange for compensation and arrangements on later flight. But before you take that step, make sure you know the answers to the following questions:

- When is the next flight on which the airline can confirm your seat? The alternate flight may be acceptable to you. On the other hand, if the airline offers to put you on *standby* on another flight that is full, be aware of the fact that you might end up stranded.

- Will the airline provide other amenities such as free meals, phone call privileges, a hotel room, ground transportation? If not, you might be forced to spend the money they offer you for being bumped on food and lodging while you wait for the next flight.

If the airline offers you a free ticket, you should have other questions: How long is the ticket good for? Is it "blacked out" during holiday periods? Can it be applied to international flights?

Most importantly, ask if you can make a reservation and if so, how far before departure are you permitted to make it?

Involuntary Bumping

DOT requires an airline to give all passengers who are bumped involuntarily a written statement describing their rights and explaining how the carrier decides who gets on an oversold flight and who doesn't. Those travelers who don't get to fly are frequently entitled to an on-the-spot payment of denied boarding compensation. The amount depends on the price of the ticket and the length of the delay:

- If the airline arranges substitute transportation that is scheduled to arrive at your destination between one and two hours after your original arrival time (between one and four hours on international flights), the airline must pay you an amount equal to your one-way fare to your final destination, with a $200 maximum.

- If the substitute transportation is scheduled to get you to your destination more than two hours later (four hours internationally), or if the airline does not make any substitute travel arrangements for you, the compensation doubles (200% of your fare, $400 maximum).

- You always get to keep your original ticket and use it on another flight. If you choose to make your own arrangements, you can request an "involuntary refund" for the flight from which you were bumped. The denied boarding compensation is essentially a payment for your inconvenience.

Like all rules, however, there are a few conditions and exceptions:

- To be eligible for compensation, you must have a confirmed reservation. An "OK" in the Status box of your ticket qualifies you in this regard even if the airline can't find your reservation in the computer—as long as you didn't cancel your reservation or miss a reconfirmation deadline.

- You must meet the airline's deadline for buying your ticket. Discount tickets must usually be purchased within a certain number of days after the reservation was made. Other tickets normally have to be picked up no later than 30 minutes before the flight.

• In addition to the ticketing deadline, each airline has a check-in deadline—that is the amount of time before scheduled departure that you must present yourself to the airline at the airport.

Domestic Flight Rules

For domestic flights, most carriers have a deadline of 10 minutes before scheduled departure, but some set theirs as much as an hour or more prior to departure. (Many airlines require passengers with advance seat assignments to check in 30 minutes before scheduled departure even if they already have advance boarding passes. If you miss this deadline you may lose the specific seats you were promised, although not the reservation itself.

International Flight Rules

Check-in deadlines on international flights are generally as much as three hours before scheduled departure time, due partially to security procedures. Some airlines may simply require you to be at the ticket/baggage counter by this time; most, however, require that you get all the way to the boarding area.

If you miss the ticketing or check-in deadline, you may have lost your reservation and your right to compensation if the flight is oversold.

Other Rules and Restrictions May Apply...

As noted above, no compensation is due if the airline arranges substitute transportation, which is scheduled to arrive at your destination within one hour of your originally scheduled arrival time.

If the airline must substitute a smaller plane for the one it originally planned to use, the carrier isn't required to pay people who are bumped as a result.

These rules do not apply to charter flights, or to scheduled flights operated with planes that hold sixty or fewer passengers. They don't apply to international flights inbound to the United States, although some airlines on these routes may follow them voluntarily. Also, if you are flying between two foreign cities—from Paris to Rome, for example—these rules will not apply. The European Community has a rule on bumpings that occur in an EC country; ask the airline for details or contact DOT.

How to Avoid Being Bumped

The most effective way to reduce the risk of being bumped is to get to the airport early. On oversold flights the last passengers to check in are usually the first to be bumped even if they have met the check-in deadline. Allow extra time; assume that the airport access road is backed up, the parking lot is full and there is a long line at the check-in counter. However, if you arrive so early that your airline has another flight to your destination leaving before the one that you are booked on, either switch to the earlier flight or don't check your baggage until after the first flight leaves. If you check your bags right away, they might be put on the earlier flight and remain unattended at your destination airport for hours.

The Big Payoff

Airlines may offer free transportation on future flights in place of a check for denied boarding compensation. However, if you are bumped involuntarily, you have the right to insist on a check if that is your preference. Once you cash the check (or accept the free flight), you will probably lose the right to demand more money from the airline later on. However, if being bumped costs you more money than the airline will pay you at the airport, you can try to negotiate a higher settlement with their complaint department. If this doesn't work, you

usually have 30 days from the date on the check to decide if
you want to accept the amount of the check.

You are always free to decline the check and take the airline to court to try to obtain more compensation. The government's denied boarding regulation spells out the airline's
minimum obligation to people they bump involuntarily.

Play Fair

Don't be a "no-show." If you are holding confirmed
reservations that you don't plan to use, notify the airline. If
you don't, they will cancel all onward or return reservations
on your trip.

10

MAXIMIZE YOUR
FREQUENT FLYER EARNINGS

Frequent flyer programs were started in the 1980's by the major airlines who wanted to reward travelers who flew their airline—while simultaneously, encouraging them to become repeat customers.

The frequent flyer programs of all major airlines work in much the same way: For each mile you fly, you earn at least one credited mile. Once you have earned a specified number of credited miles, you may "cash them in" for benefits such as, free trips, upgrades and discounts on car rentals and hotels—and more.

Although the rewards differ somewhat from airline to airline, it typically takes 25,000 miles for your first free trip within the 48 contiguous states, and 50,000 miles for a round-trip to Europe.

Since their inception, frequent flyer programs have expanded dramatically and often include rewards for the use of "partners" (certain airlines, car rental agencies, hotels, long distance phone companies, credit cards and same- or next-day package delivery).

Despite the enormous attention the frequent flyer programs have generated, it's a fact that only 15% of all frequent flyer mileage earners actually redeem their mileage. This can be partially attributed to the complicated and often convoluted programs offered by the airlines.

Understanding Frequent Flyer Programs

When you join an airline's frequent flyer program, you will earn mileage for every flight you take on that airline. You earn mileage one time only per flight, despite the number of seats you may purchase. You may also earn money through a variety of related programs from credit cards to telephone companies.

When making a reservation, give the agent your frequent flyer number. (This can also be done *after* taking a flight, but you will have to mail in a portion of your ticket in to prove you actually paid for and took a particular flight.)

You can't pool frequent flyer mileage with friends. Furthermore, frequent flyer programs will not allow you to transfer your miles to another person in an attempt to 'pool' mileage. However, some programs allow you to transfer awards to traveling companions or relatives and a few even allow you to transfer your awards to friends! Note: you can transfer trip *awards*, not *mileage*. It is safe to say, however, that such leniency is becoming increasingly rare.

Once you have accumulated enough mileage, you may apply it towards rewards (class upgrades, free tickets, discounts etc.).

How to Enroll

Only individuals can enroll. Some programs have a minimum age requirement of at least two years of age. Some airlines have a corporate program. Pets or blocked-seat luggage are not eligible for frequent flyer credits.

In order to enroll, you may: (a) call the airline's 800 number or, (b) you can fill out the enrollment form while at the airport. Once you've enrolled, you'll receive a personal ID number along with detailed information regarding the program's rules and regulations. Note: Almost all programs are free.

Joining Multiple Programs

Join the program offered by each airline you fly. Even if you don't anticipate enough future flights on the airline to get a free trip, you may be eligible for lesser benefits. For instance, if the economy section of the plane is full, airlines will sometimes upgrade frequent flyer members.

In order to maximize your frequent flyer yield, it is recommended that you limit the number of airlines on which you generally fly.

Although you may belong to more than one program, you will *not* get credit on all programs that are partners with the one you fly.

Disenrollment if You Don't Fly Soon

Many programs require you to fly within the first nine months of enrollment; otherwise, they will close your account. Make certain you read the rules carefully.

Fly or Lose Your Earnings

Generally speaking, mileage credit accumulates from the day you join. However, some airlines have been known to accept mileage as much as one month prior to enrollment—others will back up only as much as 10 days.

If you have retained your boarding pass and ticket, your mileage may be accepted after flying but before enrolling.

Not All Flights Earn Frequent Flyer Credit

Most flights earn mileage credit, but there are sometimes limits. Limits include: some discount, consolidator or special priced tickets, some economy class tickets on partner airlines, tickets that do not have a fare published on them, bulk fare and charters, and free award travels. If you purchase a ticket, but don't use it, your account will not be credited.

The good news is that business and first class tickets often earn *bonus* credit.

Tracking Your Accumulated Mileage

Frequent flyer programs keep count in one of two ways: (a) they will send you periodic statements of credits and or withdrawals, or; (b) they may automatically issue certificates once you have flown a designated number of miles. The certificates may then be cashed in for awards.

Get into the habit of keeping your ticket receipt, boarding pass and hotel/car rental agreements for a period of time following each trip. Check the airline's mileage summary report for accuracy. If you notice a discrepancy, make copies of the documents and send the copies (not the originals) along with your full name, membership number, dates of travel, class of service and your origin and destination, to the airlines' frequent flyer program.

If there is a discrepancy and you cannot produce your ticket and boarding pass, the airline may not issue credit.

Note: If you move, be sure to notify your program, because frequent flyer statements and awards certificates are generally not forwardable.

Earning Credit via Non-Airline Purchases

Often, you can earn frequent flyer mileage by doing business with one of the airline's car rental agency or hotel "partners." When making car rental or hotel reservations, ask if they are partners with your airline.

Some frequent flyer programs stipulate that you must fly on the sponsoring airline to the location of the rental agency or hotel. Be sure to read your program information brochure.

There are new opportunities in other markets as well. If you join Netcentives' program based on ClickRewards (to enroll: http://www.ClickRewards.yahoo.com,   the   system tracks your points automatically, providing you pay for your purchases on the web by credit card.

For instance, Barnes & Noble gives 1 point per dollar spent over $50 for most purchases. Music Boulevard gives 100 points for every three CDs purchased. Office Max gives 200 points when you spend $200+ via their Internet web site: http://www.Office.Max.com.

SkyMall gives 500 points for the purchase of $100 in catalog merchandise. 1-800-Flowers gives 50 points with the purchase of selected flower arrangements and/or gifts.

Claiming Your Awards

You can claim awards in one of two ways: (a) a certificate will be automatically sent to you, or: (b) you will need to submit the claim form that is generally included with your periodic mileage summary.

Flying On an "Award" Ticket

First, inform the reservation clerk that you intend to travel on an award and give him the number of your award certificate. If you don't advise him accordingly, you may lose your reservation because there are only a specified number of seats per flight allocated to "award travel."

You may not be able to fly anytime you wish. Airlines have varying policies regarding "blackouts" and "peak seasons." We'll explain:

The quickest way to earn a free trip would be to allow the airline to decide when—season, day, time—you would fly. (If you want to take your trip during a *peak* season, you may need to have/use more mileage credit.)

Usually, the days prior to and as well as those following major holidays are blacked out. Airlines set aside only so many frequent flyer seats per flight and may not offer them at all on high-demand routes.

And remember, you cannot combine awards.

Transferring Awards

The clear majority of airlines require that flight coupons be redeemed and used by the traveler who earned the frequent flyer mileage. However, some programs will allow you to transfer awards to relatives or friends.

Upgrades and Companion Tickets

You can sometimes upgrade free economy trips for a fee—usually between $15-$125. You can also get free companion tickets, upgrades for as low as 10,000 miles, and frequent flyer special promotions.

Frequent Flyer Earnings May Expire

Awards often have an expiration date—usually one year after the date of issuance. However, some airlines have just recently announced that frequent flyer earnings will *never* expire!

Other Costs

The awards are subject to income tax, which is the responsibility of the recipient. Departure taxes may be collected on international flights. This tax is included in the price of a purchased ticket.

All programs have **RESTRICTIONS**. Read the fine print, and then call a program representative with specific questions.

Taking Advantage of Your Frequent Flyer Program

The bottom line is to keep it simple. With that in mind, we recommend the following:

- Join one or two programs and fly only those airlines. You will accumulate mileage quicker and be able to audit your mileage more efficiently.

• Be sure to choose an airline that flies to the destinations you desire, or at least one whose affiliate/partner airline travel to those destinations.

• Use the products and/or services affiliated or partnered with that airline, such as hotels, car rentals, long distance phone companies, etc.

• Fly during bonus-mile promotions.

• Read the literature mailed to you by your frequent flyer program. Such mailings often contain important advance information and/or valuable coupons.

Frequent Flyer Programs and Phone Numbers

Air Canada
U.S. 800/361-8253; Canada 514/395-0300

Alaska Airlines (Mileage Plan)
800/654-5669

Aloha Airlines (AlohaPass)
800/367-5250

America West Airlines (FlightFund)
800/247-5691

American Airlines (AAdvantage)
800/882-8880

British Airways (Executive Club)
800/955-2748

Canadian Airlines (Canadian Plus)
800/426-7000

Continental Airlines (OnePass)
800/231-0856

Delta Airlines (Frequent Flyer/Skymiles)
800/325-3999

Latinpass
800/445-2846, Internet: http:www.latinpass.com
A frequent flyer company representing nine different airlines:
Aces Airline of Columbia, Aeropostal, Avianca, COPA,
Grupotaca, KLM, SAETA, TWA, and US Airways.

Midwest Express (Frequent Flyer)
800/452-2022

Northwest Airlines (World Perks)
800/447-3757

Southwest Airlines (Rapid Rewards)
800/445-5764

Trans World Airlines (Frequent Flight Bonus)
800/325-4815

United Airlines (Mileage Plus)
605/399-2400

US Air (Dividend Miles)
800/872-4738

Frequent Flyer Partners

You will note that some partnerships shown here are one-way rather than reciprocal. As partnership arrangements change frequently, it is in your best interest to telephone the airlines you are concerned about and ask for updated information.

Aer Lingus   Delta

Aerolineas Argentinas   *none*

Aeromar   United Airlines

Aeromexico   Delta

Air Canada
Air New Zealand
Ansett Australia
British Midlands
Continental
Lufthansa
SAS
Swissair
Thai International
United
Varig

Air France
Continental
Delta

Air India   TWA

Air New Zealand   United

Air UK   KLM

Alaska Airlines

British Airways
Northwest
Qantas
TWA

Alitalia

Continental
US Air

All Nippon

Delta
US Air

Alm Antillean

United

Aloha

Canadian Air
Northwest
United
Bering Air
Penair
Reeve Aleutian Airways
ERA Aviation

Ansett Australia

Air Canada
United

Ansett New Zealand

United

Asiana Airlines

American

Austrian

Delta Airlines

British Airways

American
America West
Canadian Airlines
Alaska Airlines

British Midland	American
	Continental
	Air Canada
	United
BWIA	Continental
Canadian Airlines	American
	Aloha Air
	Lan Chile
	Air Pacific
	Qantas
	JAL
Cathay Pacific	American
China Airlines	Continental
Czech Airlines	Continental
Eurowings	Northwest
Finnair	Delta
Garuda Indonesia	Northwest
Hawaiian Airlines	American
	Continental
	Northwest
Iceland Air	TWA
Japan Airlines	American
	Canadian Airlines
Japan Air System	Northwest

KLM	Northwest
	Latinpass
	KLM Air UK
Korean Air	Delta
Ladeco Chilean Airlines	*none*
Lan Chile	Canadian Airlines
LAPA	United
Latinpass	ACES
	Avianca
	COPA
	Lacsa
	Mexicana
	NICA
	Saeta
	TACA
	US Air
	KLM
Lufthansa	United
	Air Canada
Malaysia	Delta
Mexicana	United
	Latinpass
Nat. Airlines of Chile	United
Pacific Island Aviation	Northwest
Philippine Airlines	TWA

Qantas	American Alaska, Canadian USAir
Royal Jordanian	TWA
Sabena	USAir Delta
SAS	Air Canada United
Saudi Arabian Airlines	United
Singapore Airlines	American Delta
South African Airlines	Air Canada Delta Midwest Express USAir
SwissAir	Air Canada Delta Midwest Express USAir
TAM	American
TAP	Delta
Thai Airways	United
Thai International	Air Canada

Varig   Air Canada
                                   United

Virgin Atlantic   Midwest Express

TIPS, TRICKS, AND SECRETS

Stay Over Saturday Night

Business travelers generally want to return home no later than Friday night, and they are willing to pay a higher fare for that privilege. Airlines like that.

Casual travelers, on the other hand, aren't willing to part with their money so easily. Instead, when confronted with what they consider to be excessively high fares, they simply travel less. Airlines don't like that.

So the airlines came up with a clever way to sort business travelers from casual travelers—a way that enables them to charge different fares to the same city. It's the "stay over Saturday night" concept.

They believe that if you are willing to stay over Saturday night, you must be a tourist with less money to spend, so they charge you less. What a concept!

Once you get by the seeming inequities and begin focusing instead on how much money you can save by adjusting your traveling days, the whole thing stops bothering you.

Save by Traveling mid-Week

Tuesdays, Wednesdays and Thursdays are generally the cheapest days to fly, while Fridays and Sundays are generally the most expensive.

Travel at "Off Hours"

Late night departures (those which depart around or after 10:00 P.M.) are often priced lower than other flights on the same route. If you can catch a little sleep during these so-called "red eye flights," you'll be ready to start your arrival activities a day earlier—and you'll have saved the cost of one night's stay in a hotel.

Buy Children's Fares

Normally, a child pays 3/4 of the adult rate. However, airlines are not likely to discount an already discounted fare so you'll probably find your child's fare to be the same as your own. International carriers do have children's fares, so be sure to identify the little people when you are making your reservations.

Watch for Price Wars

A price war can be started by anyone but more often than not, it will be initiated by an upstart airline that's trying to lure an established airline's customers away. Once a price war volley has been fired, the established airlines will generally match or beat whatever is out there. Sometimes these low price tickets have a long list of restrictions attached, so make sure you have all the details before you decide to make your purchase.

Book in Advance

You can get lower fares by booking well in advance of your intended departure. In most cases, the discount maxes out at 21 days, but you never know unless you ask that question of the airline as soon as you begin thinking about taking a trip.

Be Flexible With Your Schedule

The best airfare deals are often limited to certain days of the week and even particular hours of the day. After you have your initial fare quote, ask the agent if you could save money by changing your departure time somewhat. Often, you'll be surprised at how much money that little question can save you.

Search for "Enticement Fares"

This, again, has to do with planning well in advance and reading the newspaper or surfing the Internet.

Often, the airlines themselves set aside a few seats on a flight which they'll sell at an low price to lure customers into making travel plans and more specifically, contacting their particular airline. (Automobile dealers do the same thing; they call those specially priced cars "leaders.")

There is another part to this story, however. If you call too early, it's possible that the airlines will not yet have made any "leaders" available. However, as the flight date approaches and they see they have too many unsold seats, they will likely throw some "cheapies" into the arena. After all, it's better to sell a seat a make a little money than to fly it empty and make nothing.

So if you don't get a reasonable discount price when you first inquire, call periodically as the departure date approaches; you just might find a bargain.

Consider Nearby, Alternate Airports

Because the majority of travelers like to fly into JFK airport in New York City, for example, flights that terminate there sell out first. Airlines learned that if they discounted flights into nearby La Guardia or Newark airports, they could lure passengers onto those flights.

The same thing happens with San Francisco vs. Oakland, Los Angeles vs. Burbank, etc. In many cases, agents do not volunteer information about alternate airports, so make sure you bring up the subject.

Call—Even After You've Bought Your Ticket—to See if the Airline Has Lowered the Fare

It's wise to call the airline a couple of times in advance of your departure date to check out the fare. Fares change frequently and they may now be selling your flight at a lower rate than you paid for your ticket. Some airlines will refund the difference, while others won't. It's certainly worth asking.

Airlines will usually rewrite a ticket for a fee of about $50, so if the ticket price dropped $100, you still win!

Always Ask if Something Less Expensive is Available

As you might have guessed, it's not an airline's duty to tell you about lower fares available through them or other carriers. So it is always wise to ask if the agent knows of a lower fare on that airline...then hang up and do some price comparison with their competitors.

Watch for "Last Minute" Airfares

As the date of departure for a given flight approaches, airline decision-makers check their computers to see how well it has sold. If too many unsold seats remain, the airline will often "dump" those seats through consolidator-type agencies.

These agencies buy the tickets at cost or near cost, mark them up slightly and then list them in the Sunday edition of major city newspapers under *Last Minute Fares*. So whereas an airline might sell seats on a Los Angeles-to-New York flight for $750 and a consolidator (see that chapter) sells them 30 days prior for $375, the last-minute fare might be as low as $275. Not bad, providing your schedule allows for such flexibility!

Watch for "Supersaver Fares"

Some supersaver fares are so low that even if you can't stay as long as the airline requires for your round-trip, you may save money by buying *two* round-trip tickets!

London and Germany: Airfare Havens

It is often cheaper to fly to London or Germany and then find a cheap fare from there to other European, African or Middle Eastern destinations, than it is to book a flight directly to your destination from the United States. Additionally, last minute (within 48 hours) deals can be incredibly attractive.

Many European countries encourage their countrymen to travel by providing generous amounts of vacation time. With so many Europeans "on holiday," travel has become a big business in England and Germany. Competition and volume have driven down prices to selected locations.

Become a Travel Agent and Get Great Deals!

Many believe that the only way to become a travel agent is to spend a lot of time and money on training and then work 8-5 Monday through Friday in a travel agency office.

There is another way, an easier, less time-consuming and cheaper way. You can become an "outside sales representative" for some travel agencies.

With a little salesmanship, you can connect with a bonded travel agency, preferably one that sells consolidator tickets. You may want to establish a small business with a name that indicates you yourself are a travel agency—and purchase business cards and checks to prove it. (International Travel, Inc. will give you more credibility than Ralph's Plane Tickets.) The object, of course, is to be able to buy your own airline tickets at low rates—or to buy a ticket for, say, $325 and then resell it to a friend for $400.

Group Inclusive Tours (GIT)

Group Inclusive Tours involve airline seats that are purchased for a group. Such tickets are usually cheaper than full fare prices because they are sold by the airlines in volume to tour operators.

Sometimes, a tour operator cannot fill his quota and has too many tickets remaining for a given flight. That operator will then sell the extra tickets to travel agencies and the agencies sell them to the public at a discounted rate, similar to that of large group purchases.

You will find GIT tickets at some, but not all, travel agencies. Call and ask your agent if he ever has GIT tickets available.

The Hub and Spoke Concept

The hub and spoke concept has to do with the way airlines centralize their operations in certain cities.

It operates this way: An airline will select a city in which to base its mechanics, flight staff and lay-over accommodations in order to reduce operating costs. Such a site is known as its hub city. The cities to which the airline flies from there are known as spoke cities.

For Example: A ticket on "Acme" Airlines from Los Angeles to Raleigh that stops or connects in Denver (Acme's hub), would generally cost less than a direct flight between the two Spoke cities.

Major airlines continue to offer direct, non-stop flights for people who desire the convenience and time-savings of non-stop flights—those who don't mind paying a little more for that convenience.

Occasionally, you will find an airline offering *double frequent flyer mileage* to passengers flying via their hub. This is generally a promotional gimmick that can earn you a lot of frequent flyer miles for an hour or two of your time. It's certainly worth checking out if you're not on a tight schedule.

Hidden Cities

Some cities are cheaper to fly to if you pretend you are going on to another destination.

For instance, your flight might be from Los Angeles to New York City with a stopover in Washington D.C. In this case, however, you don't really intend to go to New York. So, you get off in Washington—and discard the remaining portion of your ticket.

Why? Because Washington D.C. is a "hidden city," (this is just an example for your convenience and is not necessarily a fact), so the fare is less than it would be if you booked a direct flight from Los Angeles to Washington D.C.!

This technique *can* occasionally present a problem: Airlines have caught on to this game and some have tightened monitoring considerably. So, if your Los Angeles to New York City ticket includes your return schedule and the airline has no record of your re-boarding the plane in Washington D.C., *your reservation will be canceled automatically by the airline's computer.*

There are ways around this problem. You can: (a) check-in but not get on the plane (tricky to accomplish), or, (b) book your return flight on another airline. The problem with (b) is that most good fares are based on round-trip purchases.

There is yet one more option: Option (c) involves informing the airline that you have gotten off at the stopover for "business or personal reasons" and that you want to make sure that your return flight will not be affected. The reservation operator can bypass the computers' automatic "dump the reservation" command—providing he/she buys your story.

Caution! *This ploy will not work if you have checked baggage.* Airlines will not check bags to Washington D.C. for a trip that is supposed to terminate in New York. Also, the plane will not depart if they are missing a passenger who checked bags on that flight. In fact, your bags will be off-loaded in accordance with airline industry policy.

Promotional Fares

Promotional fares are round trip airfares that have additional restrictions. The restrictions might affect: cancellation penalties, minimum or maximum length of stay, non-refundability or advance purchase requirements.

Promotional fares are sparked by an airline's need to promote a "feature" such as a new destination, a new airplane or expanded service. Or, sales might be slipping and the airline wants to promote their service to that particular destination.

With promotional fares, you can expect to save at least 20% but you must be flexible as to when you would like to travel. Promotional fares are often short-lived and come with conditions and restrictions.

Promotional fares are frequently advertised in the newspaper travel section of Sunday newspapers. By just browsing there once each week, you will likely shave a considerable amount off your travel bill.

Travel agents are frequently informed of a promotional fare before the fare is announced to the public. If you have developed a relationship with a particular travel agent, ask her/him to keep you informed of last-minute promotional tickets to the destinations you want to visit.

Tour Discardments

Often, you will see package deals that offer airfare, accommodations, car rentals and various other package perks for less than the best price you were quoted on airfare alone. These tours generally exist because of a tour company's inability to sell the volume they anticipated, so they "discard" them to the public at unbelievably low prices.

Of course, you may not want to be part of a tour. Nonetheless, you still might want to consider purchasing the package to get the great airfare, and then discarding the other "amenities." It's likely you'll still travel for less.

Lets say, for example, that a seven-day tour to Jamaica, including airfare, hotel, car rental and welcome cocktail, costs $750 and a round-trip flight costs $850. Even if you don't want the full tour package, you might well save $100 by flying with the tour!

APPENDICES

TRAVEL RESOURCES
RECOMMENDED BY THE AUTHORS

ASSOCIATIONS

The International Association of Air Travel Couriers (IATC)
Readers who are interested in flying as an air courier might want to join this organization. A modest annual membership fee buys a host of services and items:
International Features
8 South "J" Street
P.O. Box 1349
Lake Worth, FL 33460
561/582-8320
E-mail: iaatc@courier.org
Internet: http://www.courier.org

International Association of Medical Assistance to Travelers (IAMAT)
Information on how to find English-speaking physicians in foreign countries.
417 Center Street
Lewiston, NY 14092
716/754-4883
Internet: http:www.cybermall.co.nz/NZ/IAMAT

Air Travel Complaints

Department of Transportation	
	202/366-2220
Aviation Consumer Action Project	
	202/833-3000
FAA Consumer Hotline	
	800/FAA-Sure
American Society of Travel Agents	
	703/739-2782
U.S. Tour Operators Association	
	212/944-5727

TRAVEL NEWSLETTERS

Those who fly frequently like to stay informed. There's no better way than via a publication delivered to your home on a monthly basis.

The publications listed below vary in their focus. Many, though not all, alert their subscribers to airfare bargains; some focus on accommodations and dining, while others are designed to serve the needs of special interest groups.

Andrew Harper's Hideaway Report
P.O. Box 300
Whitefish, MT 59937
406/862-3480
Internet: http://www.hideawayreport.com
One-year subscription: $135
This newsletter covers domestic and international retreats.

Best Fares.com
P.O. Box 171212
Arlington, TX 76003
800/880-1234
Internet: http://www.bestfares.com
One-year subscription: $49.95
This newsletter delves into special offers and money-saving opportunities having to do with all facets of travel.

Consumer Reports Travel Letter
P.O. Box 53629
Boulder, CO 80322
800/234-1970
Internet: http://www.consumerreports.com
One-year subscription: $39
This newsletter covers all aspects of travel and has proven itself over and over again.

The Educated Traveler
P.O. Box 220822
Chantilly, VA 20153
800/648-5168 or 703/471-1063
Internet: http://www.educated-traveler.com
One-year subscription: $48
This newsletter focuses on trips with academic or cultural themes.

Entrée
P.O. Box 5148
Santa Barbara, CA 93150
805/969-5848
Internet: http://ww.entreenews.com
One-year subscription: $59
This newsletter focuses on high-end hotels and restaurants worldwide.

InsideFlyer
4715-C Town Center Drive
Colorado Springs, CO 80916
800/767-8896 or 719/597-8889
Internet: http://www.webflyer.com
One-year subscription: $36
This newsletter explains frequent-traveler offerings by airlines, hotels and car rental companies.

International Travel News
2120 28th Street
Sacramento, CA 95818
800/366-9192
Internet: http://www.intltravelnews.com
One-year subscription: $18
This newsletter provides locations, bargains, news briefs, tours, and more. Largely reader written.

Jax Fax
397 Post Road
P.O. Box 4013
Darien, CT 06820-1413
203/655-8746
Internet: http://www.jaxfax.com
One-year subscription: $15
A monthly magazine with listings of flights, tours, industry news, and travel directories. A travel industry trade magazine.

The Mature Traveler
P.O. Box 50400
Reno, NV 89513
800/460-6676
Internet: none
One-year subscription: $29.95
This newsletter is designed specifically for the 49-plus crowd.

Out & About
P.O. Box 1792
New York, NY 10114
800/929-2268
Internet: http://www.outandabout.com
One-year subscription: $49
This newsletter is designed particularly for gay and lesbian travelers.

Passport
401 N. Franklin Street, 3rd Fl.
Chicago, IL 60610
800/542-6670
Internet: none
One-year subscription: $89
This newsletter concentrates on upscale destinations, domestic and foreign. It covers hotels, restaurants and shopping.

The Shoestring Traveler
P.O. Box 1349
Lake Worth, FL 33460
561/582-8320
Internet: http://www.courier.org
One-year subscription: $29
This newsletter focuses on budget travel issues, with special focus on courier travel.

Travel Companions
Box 833
Amityville, NY 11701
800/392-1256 or 516/454-0880
Internet: http://www.whytravelalone.com
One-year subscription: $48
This newsletter includes a wealth of practical information. In the back, subscribers shop for like-minded travel companions.

Travel Smart
40 Beechdale Road
Dobbs Ferry, NY 10522
800/327-3633 or 914/693-8300
Internet: TBA
One-year subscription: $37
This newsletter aims at travelers who seek bargain-hunting tips and destination information. Each month, City Insider focuses on a major city's sites, activities, sleeps and eats.

INTERNET

The Internet, though shrouded in some hype, offers a tremendous opportunity to acquire a wealth of useful travel information previously available only in multiple books or from specialized travel agents. Now, if you know where to look, the information is instantly available at your fingertips, 24-hours a day at no cost!

If you don't have a computer or if you are unfamiliar with the Internet and its operation, your local library is the place to go. They have computers available at no charge and will even assist you in getting started.

Below are some useful web sites to check out as you prepare to make your travel plans. They are listed in alphabetical order by web address and are not ranked by the quality or quantity of their content.

Travel Information Sites

The Center for Disease Control and Prevention
Medical advise for international travel, geographic recommendations, disease outbreaks, links to additional information.
http://cdc.gov/travel/travel.html

General travel assistance
http://www.excite.com/travel

Discount rail travel across Europe; Eurail passes
http://www.eurail.com

General travel resources, airfares, forums
http://www.fodors.com

Budget travel advice
http://www.frommers.com

Travelogues, advisories, country guides
http://www.lonelyplanet.com

Frequent flyer mileage assistance
http://www.maxmiles.com

Thousands of the latest travel offers from around the world
http://www.personalpassport.com

International Student Travel Confederation
http://www.istc.org/

Travel assistance of all types; excellent map resource
http://www.randmcnally.com

Airlines, arts, entertainment, destinations, activities, travel news
http://www.travel.com

Food, maps, bread & breakfasts, weather, maps
http://www.travel.epicurious.com

Agents, lodging, airlines, islands, countries, general designations
http://travel.org

U.S. State Department travel warnings, consular information sheets, various government programs and services
http://travel.state.gov

Breaking news from the pages of USA Today, on-line reservations systems
http://www.usatoday.com/life/travel/ltfront.htm

Travel Books

Travel bookstore with travel gear, web links
http://www.distantlands.com

Travel literature, travel mysteries, guidebooks, how-to books, disabled traveler resources, travel-related organization resources
http://www.literatetraveller.com

Travel books of all kinds
http://www.travelbooks.com

Maps

Maps, atlases, mapping software
http://www.delorme.com

Map your land route
http://www.freetrip.com

Worldwide maps, travel books, magazines retail stores, web links
http://www.mapper.com

City guides, driving instructions, maps, travel information
http://www.mapquest.com

Maps, routes
http://www.mapsonus.com

Maps, city profiles, road warnings, weather, street finder
http://www.randmcnally.com

Weather

Local, regional, national, world
http://www.accuweather.com

General weather, GOLFcast, SAILcast, health advisories
http://www.intellicast.com

The Weather Channel website. national and international weather, warnings, "sporting" weather
http://www.weather.com

Currency Conversion

http://www.travelocity.com

http://www.washingtonpost.com/wp-srv/business/longterm/stocks/currency.htm

On-line Reservation Systems

Book flights, rooms, car, vacations
http://www.biztravel.com

Book flights, rooms, car, vacations
http://www.expedia.msn.com

Book flights, rooms, car, vacations
http://www.previewtravel.com

Airline tickets wholesale
http://www.traveldiscounters

Book flights, rooms, car, vacations
http://www.travelocity.com

Book flights, cars, rooms, vacations; city and airport guides
http://www.wtgonline.com

APPENDIX 2

TRAVEL ADVISORIES
AND EMERGENCY ASSISTANCE

Traveling has never been safer than it is today. Still, when you're in another country where you don't speak their language and something unfortunate happens, you need to know where to turn for help.

In this chapter, the authors have assembled a number of resources that might prove valuable to you both before and during your journey.

Travel Advisories

The U.S. State Department issues periodic Consular Information Sheets about political, health, economic, and other conditions that may affect travelers. You can obtain information by calling an automated answering system at the State Department's Citizens Emergency Center at 202/647-5225. Internet: http://travel.state.gov/travel_warnings.html

The International Airline Passengers Association publishes a quarterly newsletter entitled *IAPA World* that calls attention to dangerous travel conditions in the U.S. and abroad, and offers cautionary advice. They can be reached at 214/404-9980.

Lost or Stolen Passports

If you are traveling in the U.S. when your passport is lost or stolen, immediately telephone the Department of State Passport Services at 202/647-0518 or the nearest Passport Agency. An agency employee will register the loss and make arrangements to issue a new one, usually within two weeks.

If your passport is lost or stolen while traveling overseas, report it to the local police and the nearest American embassy or consulate. A new passport can usually be issued within 24 hours. You can speed the process if you have with you a photo-copy of the identification page of the original passport, plus three passport-size photos.

Health and Medical Concerns

Receiving medical attention from a competent doctor that speaks your language can be difficult to obtain in foreign countries. When it comes to one's health, it is always better to be prepared with as much information as possible. Below are several organizations that can help you prepare for your trip abroad.

World Health Organization Publications Center
49 Sheridan Avenue
Albany, NY 12210
518/436-9686
Internet: http://www.who.int

The International Association for Medical Assistance to Travelers (IAMAT)
This organization helps locate English-speaking physicians in foreign countries.
417 Center Street
Lewiston, NY 14092
716/754-4883
Internet: http://www.cybermall.co.nz/NZ/IAMAT

MedicAlert Foundation International
This organization connects emergency medical professionals with your vital records, 24 hours a day.
2323 Colorado Avenue
Turlock, CA 95382-2018
800/763-3428; 800/344-3226; 800/432-5378
Internet: http://www.medicalert.org

Global-Doc
Prepare for your trip by consulting with a doctor who is an expert in the health hazards of your destination country. On-call medical service, kits, supplies, prescription medicines.
877/456-2553
Internet: http://www.global-doc.com

Centers for Disease Control and Prevention (CDC)
The CDC has a 24-hour voice and fax information system. This information is arranged topically and can be listened to, faxed, or mailed to you house.
1600 Clifton Road
Atlanta, GA 30333
888/232-3228
Internet: http://www.cdc.gov

TRAVEL INSURANCE

Trip cancellation/interruption insurance covers losses if a family medical crisis or certain other emergencies force you to abandon or abbreviate a trip. Emergency medical coverage covers emergency transport or medical care—or both. Bundled coverage includes both *trip cancellation insurance* and *emergency medical coverage*.

Also available is other coverage options such as that for lost baggage.

Pre-Existing Medical Conditions

For years, most travel insurers would not cover recurrences of preexisting medical conditions. However, most major companies will now cover most preexisting medical conditions providing you buy the coverage *within seven or fourteen days of making your first payment on the trip.*

Buy Direct From the Insurer

You can buy travel insurance through travel agents, cruise lines and tour operators, but most travel authorities suggest that consumers buy from the insurers themselves.

Buying directly from the insurance company has a special benefit for those who purchase vacation packages from a tour operator. Insurance to cover a tour operator's possible default is available *only* from an insurance com-pany...not from the tour operator.

Lower Premiums for Younger Travelers

Some companies offer lower premiums for younger travelers and higher premiums for older travelers (cutoff ages are typically 55 and 70). Most companies don't, however, consider travelers' ages when setting rates.

The Cost

Travel insurance averages about 4-5% of the value of an airline ticket.

Travel Insurance Company Directory

Following is a list of some of the companies offering travel insurance today.

Access America	800/284-8300
Carefree Travel Insurance	800/323-3149
C.S.A. Travel Protection	800/348-9505
Globalcare Insurance Services	800/821-2488

International S.O.S. Assistance	800/523-8662
Travelex Insurance Services	800/228-9792
Travel Guard International	800/826-1300
Travel Insurance Services	800/937-1387
Travel Insured International/The Travelers	800/243-3174
Travelsafe	800/523-8020
Tripguard Plus	800/423-3632
Worldwide Assistance Services	800/821-2828
Wallach & Co.	800/237-6615

A New Insurance Concept

There is a new type of insurance policy available that covers much less than traditional trip insurance—but it also costs about one-third as much.

For a flat $11.98 per ticket, an Orlando, Florida travel agency sells a basic insurance policy that pays off if the purchaser misses a scheduled fight due to illness or injury to the purchaser, or to the purchaser's spouse, children or a guardian. It refunds domestic or foreign tickets up to $500 and airline change-of-ticket fees up to $75. The policy also pays up to $100 for lost baggage and $50 for baggage delay.

This insurance is available from Airline Reservations Network: 888/847-7500.

NON-FARE-RELATED TRAVEL TIPS

Have the Agent Read All Information to You

Review all flight details with the agent before you end your telephone call. Pay particular attention to flight numbers, travel dates, travel cities and—when there is more than one airport in a particular area—the airports you'll be using. Make sure the airline has your home and work telephone numbers so they can inform you of schedule changes. They occur all too frequently.

Check Your Ticket for Accuracy

Your ticket shows your flight number, departure time and date and type of reservation (class) for each portion of your journey. The word OK in the *status box* means that you're confirmed on that flight. Anything else in the status box means your reservation is not yet confirmed.

Check for 4-Digit Flight Numbers

A 4-digit number often means that you're booked on a commuter airline that has an arrangement with, or is owned by, the initiating airline. If you have any concerns, ask your travel agent for details regarding the airline, aircraft type, etc.

Check the On-Time Performance Codes for Your Flights

A one-digit code that is available from the agent tells you how often that airline arrived on time (or within 15 minutes) during the most recently reported month. For example, a " 9 " means that flight arrived within 15 minutes of its scheduled arrival time 90-99.9% of the time. Note: this applies only to U.S. airlines.

If Planning to Travel During the Holidays, Make Your Reservations Early

Flights that depart the week prior to Thanksgiving day and Christmas day can sell out a month or more in advance. The same goes for possible return flights during the week following those major holidays. So buy your tickets early. (As you might guess, airlines have little incentive to discount prices on holiday flights. That's where consolidators come in handy, but you have to time it just right to get the best possible fares.)

You Haven't "Bought" Your Ticket Until You've Paid for it

If you ask your agent to put a "hold" on a reservation for 24 or 48 hours, they will. But be aware of the fact that should the airline raise the fare during the time your hold is in effect, you'll have to pay the new price. So it's wise to complete the purchase at the earliest possible time.

There is a Risk in Having Your Tickets Mailed to You

If you book well in advance of your flight, the airline will offer to mail your tickets to you, and that's usually OK. But you should be aware that if they mail them and you don't receive them, you'll have to go through a time-consuming procedure to straighten it all out. Some agents recommend private delivery services (ex.: UPS, Fed Ex., etc.) which cost more, but have a better deliver record than the U.S.P.S.

Confirm Your Reservations Before Beginning Your Journey

Airlines frequently adjust their flight schedules and when they do, they make an attempt to telephone everyone holding a reservation on that flight to notify them of the change. But sometimes things don't quite work as they're supposed to, so you're encouraged to call a day ahead of your scheduled departure to confirm your reservation.

Even though you may have confirmed the details with the agent just before you terminated the call, you should always check to make sure the information on the ticket is correct. Incorrect data entry could result in you being scheduled on the wrong flight to a country you've never even heard of!

Bring a Photo ID With You to the Airport

Airlines request a photo ID upon check-in. International airlines expect your ticket and passport names to match as well. If your name has changed recently, bring documentation such as your marriage certificate or the court order.

Getting the Best Seats on the Plane

After first class and business class, the choices have more to do with your personal priorities. If what you want is comfortable, smooth ride, a seat over the wings should be your choice. If you want a quiet ride, select a seat as far forward as possible, but be sure to avoid the galley and the rest rooms. If you want maximum leg room, select the first row or seats near the emergency exits. Warning: avoid the last row in the section because those seats often do not recline.

APPENDIX 5

FOR THE
DISABLED TRAVELER

Note: The information contained in this chapter has been drawn from an expansive document entitled <u>New Horizons: Information for the Air Traveler with a Disability</u>, published by the U.S. Department of Transportation. The authors have chosen to include a condensed version of that document here for the purpose of enlightening concerned readers who might otherwise be unaware of its existence.

The concerned reader is strongly urged to obtain a copy of the complete document in order to become more knowledgeable regarding not only his/her personal travel rights, but also the airline's responsibilities to disabled travelers as mandated by federal law. This document may be obtained on the Internet at: http://www.dot.gov/airconsumer/horizons.htm.

Travelers with disabilities sometimes have special needs when flying on commercial airlines. To assist those passengers, Congress passed in 1986 the *Air Carrier Access Act*, requiring the Department of Transportation (DOT) to develop new regulations which ensure that persons with disabilities will be treated without discrimination in a way consistent with the safe carriage of all passengers.

The new rules sweep aside many restrictions that formerly discriminated against passengers with disabilities:

- *Air carriers may not refuse transportation to a passenger solely on the basis of a disability.*

- *Air carriers may not limit the number of individuals with disabilities on a particular flight.*

- *All trip information that is made available to other passengers must also be made available to passengers with disabilities.*

- *Carriers must provide passage to an individual with a disability that may affect his or her appearance or involuntary behavior, even if this disability may offend, annoy, or be an inconvenience to crewmembers or other passengers.*

There are exceptions:
The carrier may refuse transportation if:

- *The individual with a disability would endanger the health or safety of other passengers, or if transporting the person would be a violation of FAA safety rules.*

- *The plane has fewer than 30 seats and there are no lifts, boarding chairs or other devices available which can be adapted to the limitations of such small planes, by which to place the passenger on board. Carrier personnel are not required to carry a mobility impaired person onto the aircraft by hand.*

There may be other qualifications that apply here. Consult the original document for full details.

In addition:

- *Advance notice of the intent to travel may be required, depending upon the disability involved.*

- *Attendants to care for and assist disabled passengers may be required by the airline in the case of certain disabilities.*

- *Airports must be reasonably accessible to disabled travelers. This rule applies to most, but not all airports.*

- *Moving through the airport must be made possible and that calls for shuttle vehicles and people movers.*

Passenger information must be available to passengers with vision and hearing impairments. This regards ticketing details, scheduled departure times and gates, status of flight delays, schedule changes, check-in, change of gate assignment, and checking and claiming of luggage.

Security Screening applies equally to those with disabilities. There are, however, specific guidelines as to how the security check of a disabled passenger may be conducted.

A medical certificate from the passenger's physician (indicating that the passenger is capable of completing the flight safely without requiring extraordinary medical care), may be required of some passengers with disabilities. It is important to know, however, that a disability is not sufficient grounds for a carrier to request a medical certificate.

Additional government guidelines apply to:
Aircraft accessibility
Airline compliance procedures
Assistive devices (handling of)
Charges for accommodations (prohibited)
Communicable Diseases
Handling of mobility aids and assistive devices
In-cabin service
Mobility aids (handling of)
Personnel training
Safety briefing
Seat assignments
Service animals

Again, the authors advise the concerned reader to consult the government document for specifics.

Problem Solving
Dispute resolution procedures exist for disabled airline passengers who want to file a complaint against an airline:

- *All carriers are required to have a Complaints Resolution Official (CRO) closely available to resolve disagreements which may arise between the carrier and passengers with disabilities.*

- *Travelers who disagree with a carrier's actions toward them can pursue the issue with the carrier's CRO on the spot.*

- *A carrier that refuses transportation to any person based on a disability must provide a*

> *written statement to that person within 10 calendar days, stating the basis for the refusal.*

If the passenger is still not satisfied, he or she may pursue DOT enforcement action.

Facilities and Services

Travelers with disabilities must be provided information upon request concerning facilities and services available to them. When feasible, this information will pertain to the specific aircraft scheduled for a specific flight. Such information should include:

- *Any limitations which may be known to the carrier concerning the ability of the aircraft to accommodate an individual with a disability;*

- *The location of seats (if any) with movable aisle armrests and any seats which the carrier does not make available to an individual with a disability (e.g., exit rows);*

- *Any limitations on the availability of storage facilities in the cabin or in the cargo bay for mobility aids or other equipment commonly used by an individual with a disability;*

- *Whether the aircraft has an accessible lavatory.*

APPENDIX 6

PASSPORTS AND VISAS

Passports

A passport is required to pass through the port—i.e. to exit—the United States to travel to another nation. All states have at least one office to which you can mail your passport application. Most post offices, being federal institutions themselves, are able to advise you as to where you may obtain a passport application.

Some countries require that your passport be *valid at least six months or longer beyond the dates of your trip*. If your passport expires before the required validity, you will have to apply for a new one. Check with the embassy or consulate representing the country you plan to visit for their requirements.

Some Middle Eastern or African countries will not issue visas or allow entry if your passport indicates travel to Israel. Consult the National Passport Information Center for guidance if this applies to you.

Obtaining Passport Information on the Web
You can obtain passport information at a designated post office or from the Internet at the following address: http://travel.state.org.

How to Obtain or Renew Your Passport
To obtain a passport for the first time, or to renew a lost of expired passport, application must be made at a designated post office.

A valid (unexpired) passport can be renewed by mail. Obtain the appropriate forms at your nearest post office or download forms from the web: http://travel.state.org.

Passport Fees
The price is $60 for an adult passport or $40 for a child's passport. Payment must be by check or cash in the exact amount.

You will need proof of citizenship, a photo ID (ex.: driver's license), and two recent 2-by-2-inch photographs in black and white or color.

Passport Processing Time
The passport office tries to process applications within 3 1/2 weeks, but it can take six or more weeks during the busy summer travel season.

For an extra $35, you can request expedited service, which promises that the application will be processed and mailed within three working days of receipt by the agency.

Passport Information by Telephone
The National Passport Information Center's telephone number is: 1-900-225-5674. A fee of 35¢ per minute will be charged to your telephone for this call and it takes about seven minutes to hear all of the general information.

On weekdays from 5 A.M. to 5 P.M., you may speak with a service representative at a rate of $1.05 per minute. (A service representative can be accessed at any point during the message by dialing "0".) The service representative can tell you which post offices in your area take passport application.

If you are using a phone that cannot be billed, the same information is available at 888/362-8668 for $4.95, billed to your credit card.

Visas

A visa is an endorsement or stamp placed by an official of a foreign country on a U.S. passport that allows the passport bearer to visit that foreign country for a specific purpose: i.e. to work, visit, attend classes, or to obtain medical treatments.

Visas can be obtained by contacting or visiting the consulates of countries you intend to visit before you begin your journey. Keep in mind that if you have no visa for the first country of your journey, you could be turned away immediately upon landing there. To prevent that from happening, the check-in clerks of all international airlines check your passport for the appropriate visa (at least for your first stop) before allowing you to board the airplane.

For temporary visits such as vacations, a visa is required by every nation except Canada and about two dozen others.

When possible, visas should be obtained before proceeding abroad. Allow sufficient time for processing your visa application, especially if you are applying by mail. Most foreign consular representatives are located in principal cities, and in many instances, a traveler may be required to obtain a visa from the consular office in the area of his residence.

The addresses of foreign consular offices in the U.S. may be obtained by consulting the *Congressional Directory* in your local library. Remember, it is the responsibility of the traveler to obtain visas, where required, from the appropriate embassy or nearest consulate of the country you are planning to visit.

Sometimes, travel plans change once the journey has begun and you decide to visit additional countries for which you have not yet obtained visas. Fortunately, it is often possible to obtain visas as you travel. In many countries, it is little more than a formality which can be accomplished enroute as your train travels, for instance, from Spain to France. But as one might expect, some nations have much stricter rules that could prevent you from obtaining a visa while your trip is in progress. To avoid a possible problem, it is best to discuss the situation with a travel agent before you begin your journey.

How to Obtain a Nonimmigrant (temporary) Visa

First, determine whether the country to which you are traveling requires a visa. Some do not.

If a visa is required, you can apply at one of the 230 U.S. foreign Service posts throughout the United States. There, you must present your passport, a completed application, photograph and pay a processing fee.

Applicants must demonstrate an assurance to return to the home nation. This usually requires evidence of family or other ties.

Consular officers will review your paperwork and may or may not choose to interview you.

Next, officials cross-check your name against their "lookout lists" of people barred from entering—such as criminals and terrorists.

Providing you clear the process, your visa may be issued on the spot, or within a few days.

Immunizations

Some countries may require International Certificates of Vaccination against yellow fever. A cholera immunization may be required if you are traveling from an infected area. Check with health care providers or your personal records to ensure other immunizations (e.g. tetanus and polio) are up-to-date. Prophylactic medication for malaria and certain other preventive measures are advisable for travel to some countries. No immunizations are required to return to the United States.

Note: The authors have not included information regarding which countries require immunizations. It is suggested that you telephone the consular offices of countries you intend to visit to obtain the most current information on that subject.

An increasing number of countries have established regulations regarding AIDS testing, particularly for long-term visitors. Check with the embassy or consulate of countries you plan to visit for current information.

Fees

All international flights are subject to U.S. Immigration and U.S. Customs fees paid in advance as part of your ticket. In addition, many countries have *departure fees* that are sometimes collected at the time of ticket purchase.

APPENDIX 7

FOREIGN ENTRY REQUIREMENTS

This chapter on foreign entry requirements has been condensed from the government's full document for your convenience. Foreign entry requirements are subject to change. It is advised that you obtain detailed and current entry requirement information from consular officials of the countries you will be visiting well in advance.

Only the primary consular office for each country has been listed. By telephoning the number listed below, you may be directed to a satellite office nearer your home.

Consular Information Sheets

Consular Information Sheets are issued by the State Department for every country in the world. They include such information as the location of the U.S. embassy or consulate in the subject country, health conditions, political disturbances, unusual currency and entry regulations, crime and security information, and drug penalties.

Consular Information Sheets, Travel Warnings, and Public Announcements may be heard anytime by dialing 202/647-5225 from a touch-tone phone. They are also available at U.S. embassies and consulates abroad, and through airline computer reservation systems, or, by writing and sending a self-addressed, stamped business-size envelope to:
Office of Overseas Citizens Services
Bureau of Consular Affairs, Room 4811
U.S. Department of State,
Washington, DC 20520-4818

Internet address: http://travel.state.gov

AFGHANISTAN - Passport and visa required. No tourist or business visas are being issued in the U.S. at this time. Further information: Consulate of the Islamic State of Afghanistan in New York; 212/972-2277.

ALBANIA - Passport required. Visa not required for tourist stay up to 90 days. Further information: Embassy of the Republic of Albania at 2100 S Street NW, Washington, DC 20008; 202/223-4942.

ALGERIA - Passport and visa required. Obtain visa before arrival. Visa valid up to 90 days. Further information: Consular Section of the Embassy of the Democratic and Popular Republic of Algeria, 2137 Wyoming Ave., NW, Washington, DC 20008; 202/265-2800.

ANDORRA - (See France)

ANGOLA - Passport and visa required. Visa good for 2 years from issue date. Further information: Embassy of Angola, 1819 L Street, NW, Suite 400, Washington, DC 20036; 202/452-1042/1043. Internet: http://www.angola.org

ANTIGUA and BARBUDA - Passport or proof of U.S. Further information: Embassy of Antigua and Barbuda, 3216 New Mexico Ave. NW, Washington, DC 20016; 202/362-5122/5166/5211.

ARGENTINA - Passport required. Visa not required for tourist stay up to 90 days. Further information: Consular Section of the Argentine Embassy, 1718 Connecticut Ave., NW, Washington, DC 20009; 202/238-6460. Internet: http://www.uic.edu/orgs/argentina

ARMENIA - Passport and visa required. Visa for stay up to 21 days. Further information: Consular Section of the Embassy of the Republic of Armenia, 2225 R Street, NW, Washington, DC 20008; 202/319-2983. Internet: http://www.armeniaemb.org

ARUBA - Passport or proof of U.S. citizenship required. Visa not required for stay up to 90 days after arrival Further information: Embassy of the Netherlands; 202/244-5300.

AUSTRALIA - Passport required. Further information: Embassy of Australia, 1601 Massachusetts Ave., NW, Washington, DC 20036; 202/797-3145 or 3161. Internet: http://www.austemb.org

AUSTRIA - Passport required. Visa not required for tourist stay up to 90 days. Further information: Embassy of Austria, 3524 International Court, NW, Washington, DC 20008; 202/895-6767.

AZERBAIJAN - Passport and visa required. Further information: Embassy of the Republic of Azerbaijan, 927 15th Street, NW, Suite 700, Washington, DC 20005; 202/842-0811/0001.

AZORES - (See Portugal)

BAHAMAS - Proof of U.S. citizenship and onward/return ticket required for stay up to 8 months. Further information: Embassy of the Commonwealth of the Bahamas, 2220 Massachusetts Ave., NW, Washington, DC 20008; 202/319-2660.

BAHRAIN - Passport and visa required. Further information: Consular Section of the Embassy of the State of Bahrain, 3502 International Drive, NW, Washington, DC 20008; 202/342-0741.

BANGLADESH - Passport, visa, and onward/return ticket required. Further information: Embassy of the People's Republic of Bangladesh, 2201 Wisconsin Ave., NW, Washington, DC 20007 (202/342-8373). Internet: http://members.aol.com/banglaemb/embassy

BARBADOS - Passport required. Tourists traveling directly from the U.S. to Barbados may be allowed to enter for up to 3 months stay with proof of U.S. citizenship (original or certified copy of birth certificate), photo ID, and onward/return ticket. Further information: Embassy of Barbados, 2144 Wyoming Ave., NW, Washington, DC 20008; 202/939-9200.

BELARUS - Passport and visa required. Further information: Embassy of Belarus, 1619 New Hampshire Ave., NW, Washington, DC 20009; 202/986-1606.

BELGIUM - Passport required. Visa not required for business/tourist stay up to 90 days. Further information: Embassy of Belgium, 3330 Garfield St., NW, Washington, DC 20008; 202/333-6900.

BELIZE - Passport, return/onward ticket and sufficient funds (at least $50 per night) required. Visa not required for stay up to 30 days. Further information: Embassy of Belize, 2535 Massachusetts Ave., NW, Washington, DC 20008; 202/332-9636.

BENIN - Passport and visa required. Further information: Embassy of the Republic of Benin, 2737 Cathedral Ave., NW, Washington, DC 20008; 202/232-6656.

BERMUDA - Passport and onward/return ticket required for tourist stay up to 3 months Further information: British Embassy; 202/588-7800.

BHUTAN - Passport and visa required. Further information: Tourism Authority of Bhutan; 011-975-2- 23251 or 011-975-2-23252 in Bhutan.

BOLIVIA - Passport required. Visa not required for tourist stay up to 30 days. Further information: Embassy of Bolivia (Consular Section), 3014 Massachusetts Ave., NW, Washington, DC 20008; 202/232-4827 /4828.

BOSNIA AND HERZEGOVINA - Passport required. Visa issued by local hotel or police station. Visa must be renewed every 3 months during stay. Further information: Consulate General, 866 U.N. Plaza, Suite 580, New York, NY 10017; 212/593-0264. Internet: http://www.bosnianembassy.org

BOTSWANA - Passport, onward/return ticket, and proof of sufficient funds required. Visa not required for U.S. citizens staying no more than 90 days. Further information: Embassy of the Republic of Botswana, 1531 New Hampshire Ave., NW, Washington, DC 20036; 202/244-4990.

BRAZIL - Passport and visa required. Further information: Brazilian Embassy (Consular Section), 3009 Whitehaven St., NW, Washington, DC 20008; 202/238-2828.
Internet: http://www.brasil.emb.nw.dc.us

BRUNEI - Passport and onward/return ticket required. Visa not required for tourist/business stay up to 90 days. Further information: Embassy of the State of Brunei Darussalam, Suite 300, 2600 Virginia Ave., NW, Washington, DC 20037; 202/342-0159.

BULGARIA - Passport required. Visa not required for a stay of up to 30 days. Further information: Consular Section of the Embassy of the Republic of Bulgaria, 1621 22nd St., NW, Washington, DC 20008; 202/387-7969.

BURKINA FASO - Passport and visa required. Single-entry or multiple-entry visa valid 3 months. Further information: Embassy of Burkina Faso, 2340 Massachusetts Ave., NW, Washington, DC 20008; 202/332-5577.

BURMA (Myanmar) - Passport and visa required. Further information: Burmese Embassy (Embassy of the Union of Myanmar), 2300 S St., NW, Washington, DC 20008; 202/332-9044/5.

BURUNDI - Passport and visa required. Obtain visa before arrival to avoid long airport delay. Multiple-entry visa valid for 2 months Further information: Embassy of the Republic of Burundi, Suite 212, 2233 Wisconsin Ave., NW, Washington, DC 20007; 202/342-2574.

CAMBODIA (formerly Kampuchea) - Passport and visa required. Visa valid for a 30 day stay. Further information: Royal Embassy of Cambodia, 4500 16th Street, NW, Washington DC 20011; 202/726-7742. Internet: http://www.embassy.org/cambodia

CAMEROON - Passport and visa required. Obtain visa before arrival. Multiple-entry tourist visa for stay up to 3 months. Further information: Embassy of the Republic of Cameroon, 2349 Massachusetts Ave., NW, Washington, DC 20008; 202/265-8790 /8794.

CANADA - Passport or proof of U.S. citizenship and photo ID required. Further information: Canadian Embassy, 501 Pennsylvania Ave., NW, Washington, DC 20001; 202/682-1740.

CAPE VERDE - Passport and visa required. Further information: Embassy of the Republic of Cape Verde, 3415 Massachusetts Ave., NW, Washington, DC 20007; 202/965-6820. Internet: http://www.capeverdeusembassy.org

CAYMAN ISLANDS - (See West Indies, British)

CENTRAL AFRICAN REPUBLIC - Passport and visa required. Visa must be obtained before arrival. Further information: Embassy of Central African Republic, 1618 22nd St., NW, Washington, DC 20008; 202/483-7800.

CHAD - Passport and visa required. Further information: Embassy of the Republic of Chad, 2002 R St., NW, Washington, DC 20009; 202/462-4009.

CHILE - Passport, proof onward/return ticket required. Visa not required for stay up to 3 months Further information: Embassy of Chile, 1732 Massachusetts Ave., NW, Washington, DC 20036; 202/785-1746.

CHINA, PEOPLE'S REPUBLIC OF - Passport and visa required. Transit visa required for any stop (even if you do not exit the plane or train) in China. Further information: Chinese Embassy, 2201 Wisconsin Avenue, NW, Washington, DC 20007; 202/338-6688.

COLOMBIA - Passport and proof of onward/return ticket required for tourist stay up to 30 days. Further information: Colombian Consulate, 1875 Connecticut Ave., NW, Suite 218, Washington, DC 20009; 202/332-7476. Internet: http://www.colombiaemb.org

COMOROS ISLANDS - Passport and onward/return ticket required. Visa for up to 3 weeks issued at airport upon arrival. Further information: Embassy of the Federal and Islamic Republic of Comoros, 336 East 45th St., 2nd Floor, New York, NY 10017; 212/972-8010.

CONGO, DEMOCRATIC REPUBLIC OF THE (formerly Zaire) - Passport and visa required. Visa must be obtained before arrival. Tourist/business visa, valid 1 to 3 months Further information: Embassy of the Democratic Republic of the Congo, 1800 New Hampshire Ave., NW, Washington, DC 20009; 202/234-7690/1.

CONGO, REPUBLIC OF THE - Passport and visa required. Tourist/business visa for a stay up to 3 months Further information: Embassy of the Republic of the Congo, 4891 Colorado Ave., NW, Washington, DC 20011; 202/726-5500.

COOK ISLANDS - Passport, proof of sufficient funds, and onward/return ticket required. Visa not needed for visit up to 31 days. Further information: Consulate for the Cook Islands, Kamehameha Schools, #16, Kapalama Heights, Honolulu, HI 96817; 808/847-6377.

COSTA RICA - Passport or original U.S. birth certificate and photo ID required. Further information: Consular Section of the Embassy of Costa Rica, 2112 S St. NW, Washington, DC 20008; 202/328-6628.

COTE D'IVOIRE (formerly Ivory Coast) - Passport required. Visa not required for stay up to 90 days. Further information: Embassy of the Republic of Cote D'Ivoire, 2424 Massachusetts Ave., NW, Washington, DC 20008; 202/797-0300.

CROATIA - Passport required. Visa not required for tourist/business stay up to 3 months. Further information: Embassy of Croatia, 236 Massachusetts Ave., N.E., Washington, DC 20002; 202/588-5899. Internet: http://www.croatiaemb.org

CUBA - Passport and visa required. Further information: Cuban Interests Section, 2639 16th Street, NW, Washington, DC 20009; 202/797-8518 or 797-8609 (Spanish). U.S. citizens need a Treasury Dept. license in order to engage in any transactions related to travel to and within Cuba. Before planning any travel to Cuba, U.S. citizens should contact the Licensing Division, Office of Foreign Assets Control, Department of the Treasury, 1331 G St., NW, Washington, DC 20220; 202/622-2480.

CURACAO - (See Netherlands Antilles)

CYPRUS - Passport required. Visa not required for tourist/business stay up to 3 months. Further information: Embassy of the Republic of Cyprus, 2211 R St., NW, Washington, DC 20008; 202/462-5772.

CZECH REPUBLIC - Passport required. Visa not required for stay up to 30 days. Further information: Embassy of the Czech Republic, 3900 Spring of Freedom Street, NW, Washington, DC 20008; 202/274-9123. Internet: http://www.czech.cz/washington.org.

DENMARK (including GREENLAND) - Passport required. Visa not required for a stay up to 90 days. Further information: Royal Danish Embassy, 3200 Whitehaven St., NW, Washington, DC 20008; 202/234-4300. Internet: http://www.denmarkemb.org

DJIBOUTI - Passport and visa required. Visas must be obtained before arrival. Single-entry visa valid for 30 days. Further information: Embassy of the Republic of Djibouti, 1156 15th St., NW, Suite 515, Washington, DC 20005; 202/331-0270.

DOMINICA - Proof of U.S. citizenship, photo ID, and return/onward ticket required for tourist stay of up to 6 months. Further information: Consulate of the Commonwealth of Dominica, 820 2nd Ave., Suite 900, New York, NY 10017; 212/599-8478.

DOMINICAN REPUBLIC - Passport and tourist card required. Further information: Embassy of the Dominican Republic, 1715 22nd St., NW, Washington, DC 20008; 202/332-6280.

ECUADOR (including the Galapagos Islands) - Passport and return/onward ticket required for stay up to 90 days. Further information: Embassy of Ecuador, 2535 15th St., NW, Washington, DC 20009; 202/234-7166.

EGYPT - Passport and visa required. Tourist visa valid for 1 month. Further information: Embassy of the Arab Republic of Egypt, 3521 International Court, NW, Washington, DC 20008; 202/895-5400. Internet: http://www.interoz.com/egypt

EL SALVADOR - Passport and visa required. Length of validity of visa will be determined by Consulate. Further information: Consulate General of El Salvador, 1424 16th St., NW, Suite 200, Washington, DC 20036; 202/265-9671.

ENGLAND - (See United Kingdom)

EQUATORIAL GUINEA - Passport, and proof of smallpox, yellow fever and cholera immunizations required for a stay of less than 90 days. Visas are not required, but U.S. citizens must submit 2 visa application forms, 2 photos, and proof of sufficient funds (declaring a minimum $2,000 US) to enter Equatorial Guinea. Further information: Embassy of the Republic of Equatorial Guinea, 1511 K St., NW, Suite 405, Washington, DC 20005; 202/393-0348.

ERITREA - Passport and visa required. Further information: Embassy of Eritrea, 1708 New Hampshire Ave., NW, Washington, DC 20009; 202/319-1991.

ESTONIA - Passport required. Visas are not required for stays up to 90 days. Further information: Consulate General of Estonia, 600 Third Ave., 26th Floor, New York, NY 10016; 212/883-0636. Internet: http://www.estemb.org

ETHIOPIA - Passport and visa required. Tourist/business visa valid for stay up to 2 years. Exit visas are required of all visitors remaining in Ethiopia for more than 30 days. Further information: Embassy of Ethiopia, 2134 Kalorama Rd., NW, Washington, DC 20008; 202/234-2281/2.

FIJI - Passport, proof of sufficient funds and onward/return ticket required. Visa not required for stay up to 6 months. Further information: Embassy of the Republic of the Fiji Islands, 2233 Wisconsin Ave., NW, #240, Washington, DC 20007; 202/337-8320. E-mail: fijiemb@earthlink.net

FINLAND - Passport required. Tourist/business visa not required for stay up to 90 days. Further information: Embassy of Finland, 3301 Massachusetts Ave., NW, Washington, DC 20008; 202/298-5800. Internet: http://www.finland.org/index.html

FORMER YUGOSLAV REPUBLIC OF MACEDONIA - Passport and visa required. Tourist visa is issued at border points. Further information: Embassy of the Former Yugoslav Republic of Macedonia, 3050 K St., NW, Suite 210, Washington, DC 20007; 202/337-3063.

FRANCE - Passport required. Visa not required for tourist/business stay up to 90 days in France, Andorra, Monaco, and Corsica, and 1 month in French Polynesia. Further information: Consulate General of France, 4101 Reservoir Rd., NW, Washington, DC 20007; 202/944-6200. Internet: http://www.france.consulate.org.

FRENCH GUIANA - Proof of U.S. citizenship and photo ID required for visit up to 3 weeks. No visa required for stay up to 3 months. For stays longer than 3 weeks, a passport is required. Further information: Consulate General of France, 4101 Reservoir Rd., NW, Washington, DC 20007; 202/944-6200. Internet: http://www.france.consulate.org

FRENCH POLYNESIA (Includes Society Islands, French Southern and Antarctic Lands, Tuamotu, Gambier, French Austral, Marquesas, Kerguelen, Crozet, New Caledonia, Tahiti, Wallis and Furtuna Islands.) - Passport required. Visa not required for visit of up to 1 month. Further information: Consulate General of France; 202/944-6200. Internet: http://www.france.consulate.org

GABON - Passport and visa required. Visa for a stay of up to 4 months. Further information: Embassy of the Gabonese Republic, 2034 20th St., NW, Washington, DC 20009; 202/797-1000.

GALAPAGOS ISLANDS - (See Ecuador)

GAMBIA - Passport and visa required. Tourist/business visa for a stay up to 1 year. Further information: Embassy of the Gambia, 1155 15th St., NW, Washington, DC 20005; 202/785-1399.

GEORGIA - Passport, visa, and letter of invitation required. Further information: Embassy of the Republic of Georgia, Suite 424, 1511 K St., NW, Washington, DC 20005; 202/393-6060.

GERMANY - Passport required. Tourist/business visa not required for stay up to 90 days. Further information: Embassy of the Federal Republic of Germany, 4645 Reservoir Rd., NW, Washington, DC 20007; 202/298-8140. Internet: http://www.germany-info.org

GHANA - Passport and visa required. Tourist visa required for stay up to 30 days Further information: Embassy of Ghana, 3512 International Drive, NW, Washington, DC 20008; 202/686-4520. Internet: http://www.undp.org/missions/ghana

GIBRALTAR - Passport required. Visa not required for tourist stay up to 90 days. Further information: British Embassy; 202/588-7800.

GILBERT ISLANDS - (See Kiribati)

GREAT BRITAIN AND NORTHERN IRELAND - (See United Kingdom)

GREECE - Passport required. Visa not required for tourist/business stay up to 90 days. Further information: Consular Section of the Embassy of Greece, 2211 Massachusetts Ave., NW, Washington, DC 20008; 202/939-5818. Internet: http://www.greekembassy.org

GREENLAND - (See Denmark)

GRENADA - Passport is recommended, but tourists may enter with birth certificate and photo ID. Visa not required for tourist stay up to 3 months. Further information: Consulate General of Grenada, 1701 New Hampshire Ave., NW, Washington, DC 20009; 202/265-2561.

GUADELOUPE - (See West Indies, French)

GUATEMALA - Passport required, for a stay of up to 90 days. Further information: Embassy of Guatemala, 2220 R St., NW, Washington, DC 20008-4081; 202/745-4952. Internet: http://www.guatemala-embassy.org

GUIANA, FRENCH - (See French Guiana)

GUINEA - Passport and visa required. Tourist/business visa for stay up to 6 months. Further information: Embassy of the Republic of Guinea, 2112 Leroy Pl., NW, Washington, DC 20008; 202/483-9420.

GUINEA-BISSAU - Passport and visa required. Visa must be obtained in advance. Visa valid up to 90 days. Further information: Embassy of Guinea-Bissau, 1511 K Street, NW, Suite 519, Washington, DC 20005; 202/347-3950.

GUYANA - Passport and onward/return ticket required. Further information: Embassy of Guyana, 2490 Tracy Pl., NW, Washington, DC 20008; 202/265-6900/03.

HAITI - Passport required. Visa not required for tourist/business stay of up to 90 days. Further information: Embassy of Haiti, 2311 Massachusetts Ave., NW, Washington, DC 20008; 202/332-4090.

HOLY SEE, APOSTOLIC NUNCIATURE OF THE - Passport required (for entry into Italy). Further information: Apostolic Nunciature of the Holy See, 3339 Massachusetts Ave., NW, Washington, DC 20008; 202/333-7121, or call Embassy of Italy; 202/328-5500.

HONDURAS - Passport and onward/return ticket required. Further information: Embassy of Honduras (Consular Section), Suite 310, 1612 K Street., NW, Washington, DC 20006; 202/223-0185.

HONG KONG, SPECIAL ADMINISTRATIVE REGION - Passport and onward/return transportation by sea/air required. Visa not required for tourist stay up to 90 days. Further information: Embassy of the People's Republic of China; 202/338-6688.

HUNGARY - Passport, onward/return ticket and proof sufficient funds required. Visa not required for stay up to 90 days. Further information: Embassy of the Republic of Hungary, 3910 Shoemaker Street, NW, Washington, DC 20008; 202/362-6730. Internet: http://www.hungaryemb.org

ICELAND - Passport required. Visa not required for stay up to 90 days. Further information: Embassy of Iceland, 1156 15th Street, NW, Suite 1200, Washington, DC 20005; 202/265-6653-5.

INDIA - Passport and visa required. Visa must be obtained before arrival. Further information: Embassy of India, 2536 Massachusetts Ave., NW, Washington, DC 20008; 202/939-9806/9839. Internet: http://www.indiagov.org

INDONESIA - Passport and onward/return ticket required. Visa not required for tourist stay up to 2 months. Further information: Embassy of the Republic of Indonesia, 2020 Massachusetts Ave., NW, Washington, DC 20036; 202/775-5200.

IRAN - Passport and visa required. The United States does not maintain diplomatic or consular relations with Iran. Travel by U.S. citizens is not recommended. Further information: Embassy of Pakistan, Iranian Interests Section, 2209 Wisconsin Ave., NW, Washington, DC 20007; 202/965-4990.

IRAQ - Passport and visa required. U.S. passports are not valid for travel in, to, or through Iraq without authorization from the Department of State. U.S. citizens need a Treasury Dept. license in order to engage in any transactions related to travel to and within Iraq. Before planning any travel to Iraq, U.S. citizens should contact the Licensing Division, Office of Foreign Assets Control, Department of the Treasury, 1331 G St., NW, Washington, DC 20220; 202/622-2480. Further information: Iraqi Interests Section, 1801 P Street, NW, Washington, DC 20036; 202-483-7500.

IRELAND - Passport required. Tourists are not required to obtain visas for stays less than 90 days, but may be asked to show onward/return ticket. Further information: Embassy of Ireland, 2234

Massachusetts Ave., NW, Washington, DC 20008; 202/462-3939. Internet: http://www.irelandem.org

ISRAEL - Passport, onward/return ticket and proof of sufficient funds required. Tourist visa issued upon arrival. Further information: Embassy of Israel, 3514 International Dr., NW, Washington, DC 20008; 202/364-5500. Internet: http://www.israelemb.org.

ITALY - Passport required. Visa not required for tourist or business stays up to 90 days. Further information: Embassy of Italy, 1601 Fuller St., NW, Washington, DC 20009; 202/328-5500. Internet: http://www.italyemb.org

IVORY COAST - (See Cote d'Ivoire)

JAMAICA - Passport (or original birth certificate and photo ID), onward/return ticket and proof of sufficient funds required. Further information: Embassy of Jamaica, 1520 New Hampshire Ave., NW, Washington, DC 20036; 202/452-0660.

JAPAN - Passport and onward/return ticket required. Visa not required for tourist/business stay up to 90 days. Further information: Embassy of Japan, 2520 Massachusetts Ave., NW, Washington, DC 20008; 202/238-6800. Internet: http://www.embjapan.org

JORDAN - Passport and visa required. Further information: Embassy of the Hashemite Kingdom of Jordan, 3504 International Dr., NW, Washington, DC 20008 (202/966-2664).
Internet: http://www.jordanembassyus.org

KAZAKHSTAN- Passport and visa required. Further information: Embassy of the Republic of Kazakhstan, 1401 16th Street, NW, Washington, DC 20036 (202/232-5488.

KENYA - Passport and visa required. Visa must be obtained in advance. Single-entry visas for tourist/business stay up to 6 months. Further information: Embassy of Kenya, 2249 R St., NW, Washington, DC 20008; 202/387-6101.

KIRIBATI (formerly Gilbert Islands) - Passport and visa required. Further information: British Embassy; 202/588-7800.

KOREA, DEMOCRATIC PEOPLE'S REPUBLIC OF (North Korea) - Passport and visa required. U.S. citizens need a Treasury Dept. license in order to engage in any transactions related to travel to and within North Korea. Before planning any travel to North Korea, U.S. citizens should contact the Licensing Division, Office of Foreign Assets Control, Department of the Treasury, 1331 G St., NW, Washington, DC 20220; 202/622-2480. The United States currently does not maintain diplomatic or consular relations with North Korea. Visa information must be obtained from a consulate in a country that maintains diplomatic relations with North Korea.

KOREA, REPUBLIC OF (South Korea) - Passport required. Visa not required for a tourist stay up to 15 days. Further information: Embassy of the Republic of Korea, (Consular Division), 2320 Massachusetts Ave., NW, Washington, DC 20008; (202/939-5663.

KUWAIT - Passport and visa required. Further information: Embassy of the State of Kuwait, 2940 Tilden St., NW, Washington, DC 20008; 202/966-0702. Internet: http://www.undp.org/missions/kuwait

KYRGYZ REPUBLIC (Kyrgyzstan) - Passport and visa required. Further information: Embassy of the Kyrgyz Republic, 1732 Wisconsin Ave., NW, Washington, DC 20007; 202/338-5143.

LAOS - Passport and visa required. Further information: Consular Section of the Embassy of the Lao People's Democratic Republic, 2222 S St., NW, Washington, DC 20008; 202/667-0076. Internet: http://www.laoembassy.com

LATVIA - Passport required. Visa not required for a stay up to 90 days. Further information: Embassy of Latvia, 4325 17th St., NW, Washington, DC 20011; 202/726-8213.
Internet: http://www.virtualglobe.com/latvia

LEBANON - Passport and visa required. Further information: Embassy of Lebanon, 2560 28th St., NW, Washington, DC 20008; 202/939-6300. Internet: http://www.erols.com/lebanon

LEEWARD ISLANDS - (See Virgin Islands, British)

LESOTHO - Passport, onward/return ticket, and proof of sufficient funds required. Further information: Embassy of the Kingdom of Lesotho, 2511 Massachusetts Ave., NW, Washington, DC 20008; 202/797-5533.

LIBERIA - Passport and visa required. Must have round-trip ticket and obtain visas before arrival. Tourist/business entry visa valid 3 months Further information: Embassy of the Republic of Liberia, 5303 Colorado Ave., NW, Washington, DC 20011; 202/723-0437.

LIBYA - Passport and visa required. U.S. passports are not valid for travel in, to, or through Libya without authorization from the Department of State. Application for exemptions to this restriction should be submitted in writing to Passport Services, U.S. Department of State, 1111 19th St., NW, Washington, DC 20524. U.S. citizens need a Treasury Dept. license in order to engage in any transactions related to travel to and within Libya. Before planning any travel to Libya, U.S. citizens should contact the Licensing Division, Office of Foreign Assets Control, Department of the Treasury, 1331 G St., NW, Washington, DC 20220; 202/622-2480. Application and inquiries for visas must be made through a country that maintains diplomatic relations with Libya.

LIECHTENSTEIN - Passport required. Visa not required for tourist/business stay up to 90 days. Further information: Embassy of Switzerland, 2900 Cathedral Ave., NW, Washington, DC 20008; 202/745-7900. Internet: http://www.swissemb.org

LITHUANIA - Passport required. Visa not required for a stay up to 90 days. Further information: Embassy of Lithuania, 2622 16th St., NW, Washington, DC 20009; 202/234-5860.

LUXEMBOURG - Passport required. Visa not required for tourist/business stay up to 90 days. Further information: Embassy of Luxembourg, 2200 Massachusetts Ave., NW, Washington, DC 20008; 202/265-4171.

MACAO - Passport required. Visa not required for visits up to 60 days. Further information: Portuguese Consulate, Washington, DC; 202/332-3007.

MACEDONIA- (See Former Yugoslav Republic of Macedonia)

MADAGASCAR - Passport and visa required. Visa valid within 6 months from the date of issue. Further information: Embassy of the Democratic Republic of Madagascar, 2374 Massachusetts Ave., NW, Washington, DC 20008; 202/265-5525/6. Internet: http://www.embassy.org/madagascar

MALAWI - Passport required. Visa not required for stay up to 6 months. Further information: Embassy of Malawi, 2408 Massachusetts Ave., NW, Washington, DC 20008; 202/797-1007.

MALAYSIA (and the Borneo States, Sarawak and Sabah) - Passport required. Visa not required for stay up to 3 months. Further information: Embassy of Malaysia, 2401 Massachusetts Ave., NW, Washington, DC 20008; 202/328-2700.
Internet: http://www.undp.org/missions/malaysia

MALDIVES - Passport required. Tourist visa issued upon arrival for 30 days validity at no charge. Visitors must have proof of hotel reservations, onward/return transportation, and sufficient funds (minimum of $25 per person per day). Further information: Maldives Mission to the U.N. in New York; 212/599-6195.

MALI - Passport and visa required. Visa must be obtained in advance. Tourist/business visa for stay up to 1 month. Further information: Embassy of the Republic of Mali, 2130 R St., NW, Washington, DC 20008; 202/332-2249.

MALTA - Passport required. Visa not required for stay up to 90 days. Further information: Embassy of Malta, 2017 Connecticut Ave., NW, Washington, DC 20008; 202/462-3611/2.

MARSHALL ISLANDS, REPUBLIC OF THE - Passport, sufficient funds for stay and onward/return ticket required for stay up to 30

days. Further information: Embassy of Marshall Islands, 2433 Massachusetts Avenue, NW, Washington, DC 20008; 202/234-5414.

MARTINIQUE - (See West Indies, French)

MAURITANIA - Passport and visa required. Obtain visa before arrival. Visa valid 3 months. Further information: Embassy of the Republic of Mauritania, 2129 Leroy Pl., NW, Washington, DC 20008; 202/232-5700/01.

MAURITIUS - Passport, sufficient funds for stay and onward/return ticket required. Visa not required for tourist/business stay up to 3 months. Further information: Embassy of Mauritius, Suite 441, 4301 Connecticut Ave., NW, Washington, DC 20008; 202/244-1491/2.

MAYOTTE ISLAND - (See France)

MEXICO - Passport and visa not required of U.S. citizens for tourist/transit stay up to 90 days. Tourist card is required. Tourist card valid 3 months for single entry up to 180 days at no charge. Further information: Embassy of Mexico's Consular Section, 2827 16th St., NW, Washington, DC 20009-4260; 202/736-1000.

MICRONESIA, FEDERATED STATES OF (Chuuk, Kosrae, Pohnei, and Yap) - Proof of citizenship, sufficient funds, and onward/return ticket required for tourist visit up to 30 days. Further information: Embassy of the Federated States of Micronesia, 1725 N St., NW, Washington, DC 20036; 202/223-4383.

MIQUELON ISLAND - Passport required for visit up to 1 month. Further information: Embassy of France; 202/944-6000. Internet: http://www.france.consulate.org

MOLDOVA - Passport and visa required. Further information: Embassy of the Republic of Moldova, 1533 K Street, NW, Suite 333, Washington, DC 20005; 202/667-1130.
Internet: http://www.moldova.org

MONACO - Passport required. Visa not required for visit up to 90 days. Further information: French Embassy; 202/944-6000. Internet: http://www.france.consulate.org

MONGOLIA - Passport and visa required. Further information: Embassy of Mongolia, 2833 M Street, NW, Washington, DC 20007; 202/333-7117. Internet: http://www.undp.org/missions/mongolia

MOROCCO - Passport required. Visa not required for stay up to 3 months. Further information: Embassy of Morocco, 1601 21st St., NW, Washington, DC 20009; 202/462-7734.

MOZAMBIQUE - Passport and visa required. Visa must be obtained in advance. Entry visa valid 3 months from date of issuance. Further information: Embassy of the Republic of Mozambique, Suite 570, 1990 M St., NW, Washington, DC 20036; 202/293-7146.

MYANMAR (see Burma)

NAMIBIA - Passport, onward/return ticket and proof of sufficient funds required. Visa not required for tourist or business stay up to 90 days. Further information: Embassy of Namibia, 1605 New Hampshire Ave., NW, Washington, DC 20009; 202/986-0540.

NAURU - Passport, visa, onward/return ticket and sponsorship from a resident in Nauru required. Further information: Consulate of the Republic of Nauru in Guam: Ada Professional Bldg., Marine Dr. 1st Floor, Agana, Guam 96910; 671/649-7106/7107.

NEPAL - Passport and visa required. Further information: Royal Nepalese Embassy, 2131 Leroy Pl., NW, Washington, DC 20008; 202/667-4550. Internet: http://www.undp.org/missions/nepal

NETHERLANDS - Passport required. Visa not required for tourist/business visit up to 90 days. Tourists may be asked to show onward/return ticket, proof of sufficient funds and health insurance coverage, and that there is adequate housing available for length of stay. Further information: Embassy of the Netherlands, 4200 Linnean Ave., NW, Washington, DC 20008; 202/244-5300.

NETHERLANDS ANTILLES (Islands include Bonaire, Curacao, Saba, Statia, St. Maarten) - Passport or proof of U.S. citizenship (i.e. certified birth certificate or voter registration card with photo I.D.) required. Visa not required for stay up to 14 days. Tourists may be asked to show onward/return ticket or proof of sufficient funds for stay. Further information: Embassy of the Netherlands, 4200 Linnean Ave., NW, Washington, DC 20008; 202/244-5300.

NEW CALEDONIA - (See French Polynesia)

NEW ZEALAND - Passport and arrival card (to be completed upon arrival) required. Visa not required for tourist stay up to 90 days, must have onward/return ticket, visa for next destination and proof of sufficient funds. Further information: Embassy of New Zealand, 37 Observatory Circle, NW, Washington, DC 20008; 202/328-4800. Internet: http://www.emb.com/nzemb

NICARAGUA - Passport valid 6 months beyond duration of stay, onward/return ticket and $5 entry fee required for a stay up to 30 days. Further information: Consulate of Nicaragua, 1627 New Hampshire Ave., NW, Washington, DC 20009;202/939-6531/32.

NIGER - Passport and visa required. Visa must be used within 3 months of issuance. Further information: Embassy of the Republic of Niger, 2204 R St., NW, Washington, DC 20008; 202/483-4224.

NIGERIA - Passport and visa required. Further information: Embassy of the Republic of Nigeria, 2201 M St., NW, Washington, DC 20037; 202/822-1500/1522.

NIUE - Passport, onward/return ticket, and confirmed hotel accommodations required. Visa not required for stay up to 30 days. Further information: Embassy of New Zealand; 202/328-4800.

NORFOLK ISLAND - Passport and visa required. Visa issued upon arrival for visit up to 30 days. Australian transit visa must also be obtained in advance for travel to Norfolk Island. For both visas, consult the Australian Embassy; 202/797-3000.
Internet: http://www.austemb.org

NORWAY - Passport required. Visa not required for stay up to 90 days. Further information: Royal Norwegian Embassy, 2720 34th St., NW, Washington, DC 20008; 202/333-6000.

OMAN - Passport and visa required. Tourist/business visas for multiple-entry issued for stay up to 6 months and valid for 2 years. Further information: Embassy of the Sultanate of Oman, 2535 Belmont Rd., NW, Washington, DC 20008; 202/387-1980/81/82.

PAKISTAN - Passport and visa required. Visa must be obtained before arrival. Further information: Consular Section of the Embassy of Pakistan, 2315 Massachusetts Ave., NW, Washington, DC 20008; 202/939-6295/61. Internet: http://www.pakistan-embassy.com

PALAU, THE REPUBLIC OF - Passport or proof of U.S. citizenship, and onward/return ticket required for stay up to 30 days. Further information: Representative Office, 1150 18th St., NW, Suite 750, Washington, DC 20036; 202/452-6814.

PANAMA - Passport or proof of U.S. citizenship and photo ID, tourist card or visa, and onward/return ticket required. Visa and tourist card valid 30 days. Further information: Embassy of Panama, 2862 McGill Terrace, NW, Washington, DC 20008; 202/483-1407.

PAPUA NEW GUINEA - Passport, onward/return ticket and proof of sufficient funds required. Tourist visa for a stay up to 60 days. Further information: Embassy of Papua New Guinea, #805, 1615 Massachusetts Ave., NW, Washington, DC 20036; 202/745-3680. Internet: http://www.pngembassy.org

PARAGUAY - Passport required. Visa not required for tourist/business stay up to 90 days. Further information: Embassy of Paraguay, 2400 Massachusetts Ave., NW, Washington, DC 20008; 202/483-6960.

PERU- Passport required. Visa not required for tourist stay up to 90 days. Tourists need onward/return ticket. Further information: Consulate General of Peru, 1625 Massachusetts Ave., NW, 6th Floor, Washington, DC 20036; 202/462-1084.

PHILIPPINES - Passport and onward/return ticket required. For entry by Manila International Airport, visa not required for transit/tourist stay up to 21 days. Further information: Embassy of the Philippines, 1600 Massachusetts Ave., NW, Washington, DC 20036; 202/467-9300. Internet: http://us.sequel.net/RpinUS

POLAND - Passport (must be valid at least 12 months past date of entry) required. Visa not required for stay up to 90 days. Visitors must register at hotel or with local authorities within 48 hours after arrival. Further information: Embassy of the Republic of Poland (Consular Division), 2224 Wyoming Ave., NW, Washington, DC 20008; 202/232-4517. Internet: http://www.polishworld.com/polemb

PORTUGAL (Includes travel to the Azores and Madeira Islands.) - Passport required. Visa not required for visit up to 60 days. Further information: Embassy of Portugal, 2310 Tracy Place, NW, Washington, DC 20008; 202/332-3007.

QATAR - Passport and visa required. Business visitors, tourists, those attending scientific or cultural symposia, and medical visitors are granted a 10-year multiple-entry visa at the Embassy in Washington, DC. Further information: Embassy of the State of Qatar, Suite 200, 4200 Wisconsin Ave., NW, Washington, DC 20016; 202/274-1600.

REUNION - (See France)

ROMANIA - Passport required. Visa not required for a stay up to 30 days. Further information: Embassy of Romania, 1607 23rd St., NW, Washington, DC 20008; 202/332-4851.
Internet: http://www.embassy.org/romania

RUSSIA - Passport, visa, and, in some cases, an original birth certificate required. Further information: Consular Section of the Embassy of Russia, 2641 Tunlaw Road, NW, Washington, DC 20007; 202/939-8907/8918. Internet: http://www.russianembassy.org

RWANDA - Passport and visa required. Single-entry visa for stay up to 1 month. Further information: Embassy of the Republic of Rwanda, 1714 New Hampshire Ave., NW, Washington, DC 20009; 202/232-2882.

SAINT KITTS AND **NEVIS** - Passport or proof of U.S. citizenship, photo ID and onward/return ticket required for stay up to 3 months. Further information: Embassy of St. Kitts and Nevis, OECS Building, 3216 New Mexico Ave., NW, Washington, DC 20016; 202/686-2636.

SAINT LUCIA - Passport (or proof of U.S. citizenship and photo ID) and return/onward ticket required for stay up to 6 months. Further information: Embassy of Saint Lucia, 3216 New Mexico Ave., Washington, DC 20016; 202/364-6792.

ST. MARTIN (ST. MAARTEN) - (See West Indies, French or Netherlands Antilles)

ST. PIERRE - Passport and proof of onward/return transportation required for a stay up to 1 month. Visa required for longer stays. Further information: Embassy of France; 202/944-6000. Internet: http://www.france.consulate.org

SAINT VINCENT AND **THE GRENADINES** - Proof of U.S. citizenship, photo ID, and onward/return ticket and/or proof of sufficient funds required for tourist stay up to 6 months. Further information: Embassy of Saint Vincent and the Grenadines, 3216 New Mexico Ave., Washington, DC 20016; 202/364-6730.

SAMOA - Passport and onward/return ticket required. Visa not required for stay up to 30 days. Further information: Independent State of Samoa Mission to the U.N., 820 2nd Avenue, Suite 800, New York, NY; 212/599-6196.

SAN MARINO - Passport required. Visa not required for tourist stay up to 90 days. Further information: Honorary Consulate of the Republic of San Marino, 1899 L St., NW, Suite 500, Washington, DC 20036; 202/223-3517.

SAO TOME AND **PRINCIPE** - Passport and visa required. Further information: Permanent Mission of Sao Tome and Principe to the U.N., 400 Park Avenue, 7th Floor, New York, NY 10022; 212/317-0533.

SAUDI ARABIA - Passport and visa required. (Tourist visas are not available for travel to Saudi Arabia.) Transit visa valid 24 hours for stay in airport at no charge (need onward/return ticket). Further information: Royal Embassy of Saudi Arabia, 601 New Hampshire Ave., NW, Washington, DC 20037; 202/944-3126.
Internet: http://www.saudi.net

SCOTLAND - (See United Kingdom)

SENEGAL - Passport required. Visa not needed for stay up to 90 days. U.S. citizens need onward/return ticket. Further information: Embassy of the Republic of Senegal, 2112 Wyoming Ave., NW, Washington, DC 20008; 202/234-0540.

SERBIA AND **MONTENEGRO** - Passport and visa required. The United States has suspended operations in Serbia-Montenegro and there is no U.S. diplomatic presence to assist U.S. citizens. Travel by U.S. citizens is not recommended.

SEYCHELLES - Passport, onward/return ticket and proof of sufficient funds required. Visa issued upon arrival for stay up to 1 month at no charge. Further information: Permanent Mission of Seychelles to the U.N., 800 Second Ave., Suite 400, New York, NY 10017; 212/687-9766.

SIERRA LEONE - Passport and visa required. Single-entry visa valid for 3 months. Further information: Embassy of Sierra Leone, 1701 19th St., NW, Washington, DC 20009; 202/939-9261.

SINGAPORE - Passport and onward/return ticket required. Visa not required for tourist/business stay up to 30 days, extendible to 3 months maximum. Further information: Embassy of Singapore, 3501 International Place, NW, Washington, DC 20008; 202/537-3100.

SLOVAK REPUBLIC - Passport required. Visa not required for a stay up to 30 days. Further information: Embassy of the Slovak Republic, 2201 Wisconsin Ave., NW, Suite 250, Washington, DC 20007; 202/965-5160 ext. 270. Internet: http://www.slovakemb.com

SLOVENIA - Passport required. Visa not required for business/tourist stay up to 90 days. Further information: Embassy of the Republic of Slovenia, 1525 New Hampshire Ave., NW, Washington, DC 20036; 202/667-5363.

SOLOMON ISLANDS - Passport, onward/return ticket and proof of sufficient funds required. Visitors permit issued on arrival for stay up to 2 months in 1-year period. Further information: British Embassy; 202/588-7800.

SOMALIA - Passport required. Further information: Consulate of the Somali Democratic Republic in New York; 212/688-9410.

SOUTH AFRICA - Passport required. Tourist or business visa not required for stay up to 90 days. Further information: Embassy of South Africa's Consular Office, 3051 Massachusetts Ave., NW, Washington, DC 20016; 202/966-1650.
Internet: http://www.southafrica.net

SPAIN - Passport required. Visa not required for tourist or business stays up to 90 days. Further information: Embassy of Spain, 2375 Pennsylvania Ave., NW, Washington, DC 20037; 202/452-0100 and 202/728-2330. Internet: http://www.undp.org/missions/spain

SRI LANKA - Passport, onward/return ticket and proof of sufficient funds ($15 per day) required. Tourist visa not required for stay up to 90 days. Further information: Embassy of Sri Lanka, 2148 Wyoming Ave., NW, Washington, DC 20008; 202/483-7954.

SUDAN - Passport and visa required. Visa must be obtained in advance and visas are only issued at the Consulate General in New York. Visas not granted to passports showing Israeli visas. Embassy of the Republic of the Sudan, 2210 Massachusetts Ave., NW, Washington, DC 20008; 202/338-8565/8570. Internet: http://www.sudline.net

SURINAME - Passport and visa required. Further information: Embassy of the Republic of Suriname, Suite 108, 4301 Connecticut Ave., NW, Washington, DC 20008; 202/244-7488/7490.

SWAZILAND - Passport required. Visa not required for stay up to 60 days. Further information: Embassy of the Kingdom of Swaziland, 3400 International Dr., NW, Suite 3M, Washington, DC; 202/362-6683.

SWEDEN - Passport required. Visa not required for a stay up to 90 days. Further information: Embassy of Sweden, 1501 M St., NW, Washington, DC 20005-1702; 202/467-2600.
Internet: http://www.swedenemb.org

SWITZERLAND - Passport required. Visa not required for tourist/business stay up to 90 days. Further information: Embassy of Switzerland, 2900 Cathedral Ave., NW, Washington, DC 20008; 202/745-7900. Internet: http://www.swissemb.org

SYRIA - Passport and visa required. Obtain visa in advance. Single-entry and multiple-entry visas valid for 3 months. Further information: Embassy of the Syrian Arab Republic, 2215 Wyoming Ave., NW, Washington, DC 20008; 202/232-6313.

TAHITI - (See French Polynesia)

TAIWAN - Passport required. Visa not required for stay up to 14 days. Further information: Taipei Economic and Cultural Representative Office, 4201 Wisconsin Avenue, NW, Washington, DC 20016-2137; 202/895-1800. Internet: http://www.taipei.org

TAJIKISTAN - Passport and visa required. At the time of publication, the Russian Consulate was handling visas. The visa process must be initiated in Tajikistan by the sponsoring agency or by the travel agent involved; no visa request is initiated at the Russian Consulate. Visas are not issued until an approval cable arrives from the Ministry of Foreign Affairs in Tajikistan to the Russian Consulate. Further information: Consular Section of the Embassy of Russia, 1825 Phelps Pl., NW, Washington, DC 20008; 202/939-8907/8913/8918.

TANZANIA - Passport and visa required. Obtain visa before departure. Visas for mainland Tanzania are valid for Zanzibar. Business/tourist visa valid 6 months from date of issuance for 1 entry up to

30 days. Further information: Embassy of the United Republic of Tanzania, 2139 R St., NW, Washington, DC 20008; 202/939-6125.

THAILAND - Passport and onward/return ticket required. Tourist visa not required for stay up to 30 days. Further information: Royal Thai Embassy, 1024 Wisconsin Ave., NW, Washington, DC 20007; 202/944-3608. Internet: http://www.thaiembdc.org

TOGO - Passport and visa required. Further information: Embassy of the Republic of Togo, 2208 Massachusetts Ave., NW, Washington, DC 20008; 202/234-4212/3.

TONGA - Passport and onward/return ticket required. Visa not required for stay up to 30 days. Further information: Consulate General of Tonga, 360 Post St., Suite 604, San Francisco, CA 94108; 415/781-0365.

TRINIDAD AND **TOBAGO** - Passport required. Visa not required for tourist/business stay up to 3 months. Further information: Embassy of Trinidad and Tobago, 1708 Massachusetts Ave., NW, Washington, DC 20036; 202/467-6490.

TUNISIA - Passport and onward/return ticket required. Visas not required for tourist/business stay up to 4 months. Further information: Embassy of Tunisia, 1515 Massachusetts Ave., NW, Washington, DC 20005; 202/862-1850.

TURKEY - Passport and visa required. Visas can be obtained at Turkish border crossing points for tourist/business visits up to 3 months or through a Turkish consular office in the U.S. or overseas. Further information: Embassy of the Republic of Turkey, 1714 Massachusetts Ave., NW, Washington, DC 20036; 202/659-0742. Internet: http://www.turkey.org

TURKMENISTAN - Passport and visa required. Further information: Embassy of Turkmenistan, 2207 Massachusetts Ave., NW, Washington, DC 20008; 202/588-1500.
Internet: http://www.embassyofturkmenistan.org

TURKS AND **CAICOS** - (See West Indies, British)

TUVALU - Passport and onward/return ticket and proof of sufficient funds required. Visitors permit issued on arrival. Further information: British Embassy; 202/588-7800.

UGANDA - Passport and visa required. Further information: Embassy of the Republic of Uganda, 5911 16th St., NW, Washington, DC 20011/202/726-7100-02.

UKRAINE - Passport and visa required. Further information: Embassy of Ukraine, 3350 M St., NW, Washington, DC 20007; 202/333-7507/08/09. Internet: http://www.ukremb.com

UNITED ARAB EMIRATES - Passport and visa required. Single-entry visa valid within 2 months from the date of issuance for stay up to 30 days at no charge. Multiple-entry visa (for business only), valid 1 to 10 years from date of issue for maximum stay of 6 months per entry at no charge. Transit visa must be obtained in advance (through travel agency, hotel, or company in UAE), and is valid for a stay up to 15 days. Further information: Embassy of the United Arab Emirates, 3000 K St., NW, Washington, DC 20007; 202/338-6500.

UNITED KINGDOM (England, Northern Ireland, Scotland, and Wales) - Passport required. Visa not required for stay up to 6 months. Further information: Consular Section of the British Embassy, 19 Observatory Circle, NW, Washington, DC 20008; 202/588-7800. Internet: http://www.britain-info.org

URUGUAY - Passport required. Visa not required for stay up to 3 months. Further information: Embassy of Uruguay, 1918 F St., NW, Washington, DC 20008; 202/331-4219.
Internet: http://www.embassy.org/uruguay

UZBEKISTAN - Passport and visa required. Further information: Embassy of the Republic of Uzbekistan , 1746 Massachusetts Ave., NW, 20036; 800/734-4078.

VANUATU - Passport and onward/return ticket required. Visa not required for stay up to 30 days. Further information: U.N. Mission; 212/593-0144.

VATICAN - (See Holy See)

VENEZUELA - Passport and tourist card required. Tourist card can be obtained from airlines serving Venezuela. Visa valid 90 days at no charge. Further information: Consular Section of the Embassy of Venezuela, 1099 30th Street, NW, Washington, DC 20007; 202/342-2214. Internet: http://www.emb.avenez-us.gov

VIETNAM - Passport and visa required. Tourist/business visa valid for 6 months. Visa authorization is arranged by sponsor in Vietnam and the Embassy cannot process visas until it receives authorization or approval from Vietnam. Further information: Embassy of Vietnam, 1233 20th St., NW, Suite 400, Washington, DC 20036; 202/861-2293 or 202/861-0694. Internet: http://www.vietnamembassy-usa.org.

VIRGIN ISLANDS, BRITISH (Islands include Anegarda, Jost van Dyke, Tortola and Virgin Gorda) - Proof of U.S. citizenship, photo ID, onward/return ticket and sufficient funds required for tourist stay up to 6 months. Further information: British Embassy for further information; 202/588-7800.

WALES - (See United Kingdom)

WEST INDIES, BRITISH (Islands include Anguilla, Montserrat, Cayman Islands, Turks and Caicos) - Proof of U.S. citizenship, photo ID, onward/return ticket and sufficient funds required for tourist stay up to 6 months. Further information: British Embassy for further information; 202/588-7800.

WEST INDIES, FRENCH (Islands include Guadeloupe, Isles des Saintes, La Desirade, Marie Galante, Saint Barthelemy, St. Martin and Martinique) - Proof of U.S. citizenship and photo ID required for visit up to 3 weeks. No visa required for stay up to 3 months. For stays longer than 3 weeks, a passport is required. For stays longer than 3 weeks, a passport is required Embassy of France; 202/944-6200. Internet: http://www.france.consulate.org

WESTERN SAMOA - (See Samoa)

YEMEN, REPUBLIC OF - Passport and visa required. Visa valid 30 days from date of issuance. Entry not granted to passports showing Israeli visas. Further information: Embassy of the Republic of Yemen, Suite 705, 2600 Virginia Ave., NW, Washington, DC 20037; 202/965-4760.

ZAIRE - (See Congo, Democratic Republic of)

ZAMBIA - Passport and visa required. Obtain visa in advance. Tourist/business multiple-entry visa, valid up to 3 years. Further information: Embassy of the Republic of Zambia, 2419 Massachusetts Ave., NW, Washington, DC 20008; 202/265-9717.

ZANZIBAR - (See Tanzania)

ZIMBABWE - Passport, visa, onward/return ticket and proof of sufficient funds required for a stay up to 3 months. Visas issued upon arrival in Zimbabwe. Further information: Embassy of Zimbabwe, 1608 New Hampshire Ave., NW, Washington, DC 20009; 202/332-7100.

AIRLINE TELEPHONE NUMBERS AND INTERNET ADDRESSES

Major Airlines

Here is a list including most of the major airlines of the world complete with telephone and Internet addresses.

AccessAir   877/462-2237
    http://www.accessair.com

Aces Airline of Colombia   800/846-2237
    http://www.acescolombia.com

Aer Lingus   800/223-6537
    http://www.aerlingus.ie

Aero California   800/237-6225
    No web site

Aeroflot Russian Int'l.   800/995-5555
   http://www.aeroflot.org/index.htm

Aerolineas Argentinas   305/333-0267
   http://www.aerolineas.com

Aeromexico   800/237-6639
   http://www.aeromexico.com

Air Aruba   800/882-7822
   http://www.airaruba.com

Air Canada   800/776-3000
   http://www.aircanada.ca

Air China   212/371-9898
   http://www.airchina.com.cn

Air Europa   800/238-7672
   http://www.easyspain.com

Air France   800/237-2747
   http://www.airfrance.com

Air Gabon   212/447-6700
   http://www.saritel.it/discloc/dst-info-gn.html

Air India   212/751-6200
   http://www.airindia.com

Air Jamaica   800/523-5585
   http://www.airjamaica.com

Air Lanka   800/247-5265
   http://www.airlanka.com

Air New Zealand http://www.airnz.com	800/262-1234
Air Pacific http://www.airpacific.com	800/227-4446
Air St. Thomas http://www.airstthomas.com	800/522-3084
AirTran http://www.airtran.com	800/825-8538
Air UK (KLM) http://www.klmuk.com	800/249-2478
Air Zimbabwe http://www.airzimbabwe.com	800/228-9485
Alaska Airlines http://www.alaska-air.com	800/426-0333
Alitalia http://www.alitalia.com	800/223-5730
Aloha Airlines http://www.alohaair.com	800/367-5250
ALM (Antillean Airlines) http://www.airalm.com	800/327-7197
American Airlines http://aa.com	800/433-7300
American Eagle http://aa.com	800/433-7300

American Trans Air http://www.ata.com	800/225-2995
America West Airlines http://www.americawest.com	800/235-9292
ANA (All Nippon Airways) http://www.ana.co.jp	800/235-9262
AOM French Airlines http://www.flyaom.com	800/892-9136
Ansett Australia Airlines http://www.airnz.com	800/366-1300
Asiana Airlines http://www.flyasiana.com	800/227-4262
Atlantic Airlines http://www.atlanticairlines.com	800/879-0000
Austrian Airlines http://www.austrianair.com	800/843-0002
Avensa-Servivensa S.A. http://www.avensa.com	800/428-3672
Avianca Airlines http://www.avianca.com.co	800/284-2622
Aviateca de Guatemala http://www.grupotaca.com	800/327-9832
Bahamasair http://www.bahamasair.com	800/222-4262

Bailair/CTA No web site	800/322-5247
Balkan Bulrarian Airlines http://www.balkan.com	800/776-5706
British Airways http://www.british-airways.com	800/247-9297
British Midland http://www.iflybritishmidland.com	800/788-0555
BWIA International http://www.bwee.com	800/538-2942
Canadian Airlines International http://www.cdnair.ca	800/426-7000
Cape Air (USA) http://www.flycapeair.com	800/352-0714
Cathay Pacific http://www.cathay-usa.com	800/233-2742
Cayman Airways http://www.caymanairways.com	800/422-9626
China Airlines http://www.china-airlines.com	800/227-5118
China Eastern Airlines http://www.ce-air.com	800/200-5118
China Southern Airlines http://www.cs-air.com	323/653-8088

City Bird   888/248-9247
http://www.citybird.com

Comair   800/354-9822
http://www.fly-comair.com

Continental Airlines   800/525-0280
http://www.flycontinental.com

COPA Airlines   800/359-2672
http://www.copaair.com

Corporate Express   800/555-6565
No web site

Czech Airlines (CSA)   800/223-2365
http://www.csa.cz

Cyprus Airways, Ltd.   877/359-6629
http://www.cyprusair.com.cy

Delta Airlines   800/221-1212
http://www.delta-air.com

Delta Express   800/325-5205
http://www.delta-air.com/express/index.html

Eastwind   800/644-3592
http://www.eastwindairlines.com

Egyptair   800/334-6787
http://www.egyptair.com.eg

El Al Israel Airlines   800/223-6700
http://www.elal.co.il

Ethopian Airlines   800/445-2733
    No web site

Finnair   800/950-5000
    http://www.us.finnair.com

Frontier   800/432-1359
    http://www.flyfrontier.com

Garuda Indonesia   800/342-7832
    http://www.garudausa.com

Grand Canyon Airlines   800/528-2413
    http://www.grandcanyonairlines.com

Gulf Air Company   800/553-2824
    http://www.gulfairco.com

Gulfstream   800/525-0280
    http://www.gulfstreamair.com

Guyana Airways   718/523-2300
    No web site

Hawaiian Airlines (USA)   800/367-5320
    http://www.hawaiianair.com

Horizon Air   800/547-9308
    http://www.horizonair.com

Iberia Airlines   800/772-4642
    http://www.iberia.com

Icelandair   800/223-5500
    http://www.icelandair.is

Japan Airlines (JAL)   800/525-3663
    http://www.japanair.com

Kenya Airways   800/343-2506
    http://www.kenyaairway.co.uk

KLM Royal Dutch Airlines   800/374-7747
    http://www.klm.com

Korean Air   800/438-5000
    http://www.koreanair.com

Kuwait Airways   800/458-9248
    http://www.kuwait-airways.com

LACSA Airlines   800/225-2272
    http://www.grupotaca.com

Lan-Chile Airways   800/735-5526
    http://www.lanchile.com

Lloyd Aero Boliviano   800/327-7407
    http://labairlines.bo.net

Lot-Polish Airlines   800/223-0593
    http://www.lot.com

LTU International Airways   800/888-0200
    http://www.ltu.com

Lufthansa German Airlines   800/645-3880
    http://www.lufthansa.com

Malaysia Airlines   800/552-9264
    http://www.malaysiaairlines.com

Malev Hungarian Airline http://www.malev.hu	800/223-6884
Martinair Holland http://www.martinair.com	800/627-8462
Mesa Airlines http://www.mesa-air.com	800/637-2247
MetroJet http://www.flymetrojet.com	888/638-7653
Mexicana Airlines http://www.mexicana.com	800/531-7921
Midway http://www.midwayair.com	800/446-4392
Midwest Express http://www.midwestexpress.com	800/452-2022
Mountain Air Express http://www.mountainairexpress.com	800/788-4247
Myrtle Beach Jet Express http://www.myrtlebeachjetexp.com	800/386-2786
New Frontiers http://www.newfrontiers.com	800/677-0720
Nica Airlines http://www.grupotaca.com	800/831-6422
Northwest Airlines http://www.nwa.com	800/225-2525

Olympic Airways   800/223-1226
  http://agn.hol.gr

Pan American World Airways   603/766-2003
  http://www.flypanam.com

Paradise Island Airlines   800/722-4262
  http://www.bahamascom.com

Pakistan International Airlines   800/221-2552
  http://www.piac.com

Phillipine Airlines   800/435-9725
  http://www.philippineair.com

Polynesian Airlines   310/830-7263
  http://www.polynesianairlines.co.nz

ProAir   800/939-9551
  http://www.proair.com

Qantas Airways   800/227-4500
  http://www.qantas.com

Reno Air   800/736-6247
  http://www.renoair.com

Royal Air Maroc   800/344-6726
  http://royalairmaroc.com

Royal Jordanian   800/223-0470
  http://rja.com

SAS - Scandinavian Airlines   800/221-2350
  http://www.sas.se

Sabena Belgian World Airway   800/955-2000
http://www.sabena.com

Saudi-Arabian Airlines   800/472-8342
http://www.saudiairlines.com

Shuttle by United   800/428-4322
http://www.ual.com

Singapore Airlines   800/742-3333
http://www.singaporeair.com

Skywest   800/742-9417
http://www.delta-air.com

South African Airlines   800/722-9675
http://www.saa.co.za/saa

Southwest Airlines   800/435-9792
http://www.iflyswa.com

Spirit   800/772-7117
http://www.spiritair.com

Sun Country   800/752-1218
http://www.suncountry.com

SunJet   800/478-6538
http://www.sunjet.com

Surinam Airways   800/327-6864
No web site

Swissair   800/221-4750
http://www.swissair.com

Taca International Airlines http://www.grupotaca.com	800/535-8780
Tap Air Portugal http://www.TAP-AirPortugal.pt	800/221-7370
Tarom-Romanian Air http://tarom.digiro.net	212/687-6242
Thai Airways http://www.thaiair.com	800/426-5204
Tower Air http://www.towerair.com	800/221-2500
Transbrasil International Airlines http://www.transbrasil.com.br	800/872-3153
TWA http://www.twa.com	800/221-2000
Trans World Express http://www.twa.com	800/221-2000
Turkish Airlines http://www.turkishairlines.com	800/874-8875
United Airlines http://www.ual.com	800/241-6522
United Express http://www.ual.com	800/748-8853
US Airways http://www.usairways.com	800/428-4322

US Airways Express http://www.usairways.com	800/428-4322
Vanguard http://www.flyvanguard.com	800/826-4827
Varig Brasilian Airlines http://www.varig.com.br	800/468-2744
VASP Brazilian http://www.vasp.com.br	800/732-8277
Virgin Atlantic Airways http://www.fly.virgin.com	800/862-8621
WinAir http://www.flywinair.com	877/494-6247

Budget Airlines

Some airlines fly to a limited number of cities and offer fares on those routes that can cost 50-60% less than what one of the major airlines would charge.

The authors thought it would be valuable to sort those airlines from the master list above for the convenience of the reader.

AccessAir   877/462-2237
http://www.accessair.com
Des Moines, Los Angeles, New York LaGuardia, Peoria and Quad cities

AirTran Airlines   800/247-8726
http://www.airtran.com
Akron, Canton, Atlanta, Bloomington, IL, Boston, Buffalo,
Chicago, Midway, Dallas/Fort Worth, Dayton, Flint, Fort. Lau-
derdale, Fort Myers, Fort Walton Beach, Greensboro, NC,
Memphis, Miami, Moline, Newark, New Orleans, Newport
News/Norfolk, New York LaGuardia, Orlando, Philadelphia,
Raleighh/Durham, Savannah, Tampa, Washington Dulles

America West   800/235-9592
http://www.americawest.com
Acapulco, Albuquerque, Anchorage, Atlanta, Austin, Balti-
more, Boston, Burbank, Carlsbad/Oceanside, CA, Chicago
Midway, Chicago O'Hare, Cleveland, Colorado Springs, Fort
Lauderdale, Houston Intercontinental, Indianapolis, Ixtapa,
Kansas City, Las Vegas, Long Beach, Los Angeles, Los Cabos,
Manzanillo, Mazatlan, Mexico City, Miami, Midland/Odessa,
Milwaukee, Ontario, CA, Orange County, Orlando, Palm
Springs, Reno, Sacramento, St. Louis, Salt Lake City, San An-
tonio, San Diego, San Francisco, San Jose, CA, San Louis
Obispo, Seattle, Tampa, Tucson, Vancouver, Washington Dul-
les, Washington National, West Palm Beach, Wichita

American Trans Air   800/225-2995
http://www.ata.com
Cancun, Chicago Midway, Dallas/Fort Worth, Dayton, Des
Moines, Denver, Dublin (Ireland), Fort Lauderdale, Fort
Myers, Grand Rapids, Honolulu, Indianapolis, Lansing, Las
Vegas, Los Angeles, Madison, Maui, Milwaukee, New York
JFK & LaGuardia, Orlando, Philadelphia, Phoenix, St. Peters-
burg/Clearwater, San Francisco, San Juan, Sarasota, Shannon
(Ireland)

Atlantic Airlines   800/879-0000
http://www.atlanticairlines.com
Baton Rouge, Beaumont, Gainesville, Gulfport/Biloxi, Houston
Hobby & Intercontinental, Jacksonville, FL, Lafayette, Lake

Charles, Lakeland, FL, Mobile, New Orleans, Orlando, Panama City, Pensacola, Tallahassee

Cape Air   800/352-0714
http://www.flycapeair.com
Boston, Fort Lauderdale, Fort Myers, Hyannis, Key West, Manteo, NC, Marthas Vineyard, Nantucket, Naples, FL, New Bedford, Norfolk, Providence, Provincetown, St. Thomas, San Juan

CityBird   888/248-9247
http://www.citybird.com
Brussels, Los Angeles, Mexico City, Miami, Orlando, San Francisco

Corporate Express   800/555-6565
No web site
Atlanta, Nashville

Delta Express   800/325-5205
http://www.delta-air.com/express/index.html
Albany, Allentown, Boston, Buffalo, Cleveland, Columbus, OH, Fort Lauderdale, Fort Myers, Hartford, Indianapolis, Islip, Kansas City, Louisville, Nashville, Newark, Orlando, Providence, Raleigh, Durham, Rochester, NY, Syracuse, Tampa, Washington Dulles, West Palm Beach

Eastwind   800/644-3592
http://www.eastwindairlines.com
Boston, Greensboro, New York LaGuardia, Orlando, Philadelphia, Pittsburgh, Trenton

Frontier   800/432-1359
http://www.flyfrontier.com
Albuquerque, Atlanta, Baltimore, Bloomington, IL, Boston, Chicago, Midway, Dallas/Fort Worth, Denver, El Paso, Las Vegas, Los Angeles, Minneapolis/St. Paul, New York LaGuardia,

Omaha, Phoenix, Portland, OR, Salt Lake City, San Diego, San Francisco, Seattle

Gulfstream   800/525-0280
http://www.gulfstreamair.com
Fort Lauderdale, Fort Myers, Freeport, Gainesville, Jacksonville, Key West, Marsh Harbour, Miami, Nassau, North Eleuthera, Orlando, Paradise Island (Bahamas), Tallahassee, Tamps, Treasure Cay, West Palm Beach

Mesa Airlines   800/637-2247
http://www.mesa-air.com
Albuquerque, Alamogordo Carlsbad, NM, Clovis, Colorado Springs, Dallas/Fort Worth, Denver, Farmington, Hobbs, NM, Las Cruces, Roswell, Silver City, NM

MetroJet   (888) 638-7653
http://www.flymetrojet.com
Albany, Atlanta, Baltimore, Birmingham, Boston, Buffalo, Chicago Midway, Cleveland, Columbus, Fort Lauderdale, Hartford, Jacksonville, Manchester, NH, Miami, New Orleans, Orlando, Providence, Raleigh/Durham, Rochester, NY, St. Louis, Tampa, Washington Dulles, West Palm Beach, Milwaukee

Midway   800/446-4392
http://www.midwayair.com
Atlanta, Baltimore, Boston, Charleston, Columbia, SC, Columbus, OH, Fort Lauderdale, Greenville/Spartanburg, Hartford, Indianapolis, Jacksonville, Myrtle Beach, Newark, Newburgh, new Orleans, New York LaGuardia, Norfolk, Orlando, Philadelphia, Raleigh/Durham, Tampa, Washington National, West Palm Beach, Wilmington

Mountain Air Express   800/788-4247
http://www.mountainairexpress.com
Burbank, Catalina, Fresno, Grand canyon, Las Vegas, Laugh-
lin, Long Beach, Mammoth, Monterey, CA, Reno, San Diego,
San Jose, South Lake Tahoe, Yosemite

Myrtle Beach Jet Express   800/386-2786
http://www.myrtlebeachjetexp.com
Myrtle Beach, Newark, Tampa/St. Petersburg

National Airlines   800/757-5387
http://www.nationalairlines.com
Chicago Midway, Las Vegas, Los Angeles, New York JFK, San
Francisco

ProAir   800/939-9551
http://www.proair.com
Atlanta, Baltimore/Washington, Chicago Midway, Detroit, Fort
Myers, Indianapolis, Newark, New York LaGuardia, Orlando,
Philadelphia, Tampa

Reno Air   800/736-6247
http://www.renoair.com
Anchorage, Chicago O'Hare, Colorado Springs, Las Vegas,
Los Angeles, Oklahoma City, Orange County, Portland, Reno,
San Diego, San Francisco, San Jose, Seattle

Southwest Airlines   800/435-9792
http://www.iflyswa.com
Albuquerque, Amarillo, Austin, Baltimore, Birmingham, Boise,
Burbank, Chicago Midway, Cleveland, Columbus, Corpus
Christi, Dallas Love Field, Detroit Metro, El Paso, Fort Lauder-
dale, Harlingen, TX, Houston Hobby & Intercontinental, Indi-
anapolis, Jackson, MS, Jacksonville, FL, Kansas City, Las Ve-
gas, Little Rock, Long Island, Los Angeles, Louisville,
Lubbock, Manchester, NH, Midland/Odessa, Nashville, New
Orleans, Oakland, Oklahoma City, Omaha, Ontario, CA, Or-

ange County, CA, Orlando, Phoenix, Portland, Providence, Raleigh/Durham, Reno, Sacramento, St. Louis, Salt Lake City, San Antonio, San Diego, San Francisco, San Jose, Seattle, Spokane, Tampa, Tucson, Tulsa

Spirit   800/772-7117
http://www.spiritair.com
Atlantic City, Boston, Cleveland, Detroit, Fort Lauderdale, Fort Myers, Islip, Los Angeles, Melbourne, FL, Myrtle Beach, Newark, New York LaGuardia, Orlando, Tampa, West Palm Beach

Sun Country   800/752-1218
http://www.suncountry.com
Anchorage, Aruba, Boston, Dallas/Fort Worth, Detroit, Houston, Las Vegas, Los Angeles, Milwaukee, Minneapolis/St. Paul, New York JFK, Orlando, Phoenix, San Antonio, San Diego, San Francisco, Seattle, Washington Dulles

SunJet   800/478-6538
http://www.sunjet.com
Fort Lauderdale, Newark, Orlando, Tampa/St. Petersburg, West Palm Beach

Tower Air   800/348-6937
http://www.towerair.com
Athens, Fort Lauderdale, Los Angeles, Miami, New York JFK, Paris, San Francisco, San Juan, Santo Domingo, Tel Aviv

Vanguard   800/826-4827
http://www.flyvanguard.com
Atlanta, Buffalo, Chicago, Midway, Cincinnati, Dallas/Fort Worth, Denver, Kansas City, Minneapolis/St. Paul

WinAir   877/494-6247
http://www.flywinair.com
Las Vegas, Long Beach, Oakland, Sacramento, Salt Lake City

AIRPORT CODES

If you can recognize the codes for the various destinations of your journey, you might be able to eliminate the possibility of the airlines sending of your luggage to an incorrect destination.

ABQ	Albuquerque, New Mexico
ACA	Acapulco, Mexico
AIY	Atlantic City, New Jersey
AKL	Auckland, New Zealand
AMS	Amsterdam, Holland
ANC	Anchorage, Alaska
ASU	Asuncion, Paraguay
ATL	Atlanta, Georgia
BAH	Manama, Bahrain
BCN	Barcelona, Spain
BER	Berlin, Germany
BHM	Birmingham, Alabama
BIS	Bismarck, North Dakota

BKK	Bangkok, Thailand
BOI	Boise, Idaho
BOS	Boston, Massachusetts
BUD	Budapest, Hungary
BUE	Buenos Aires, Argentina
BUF	Buffalo, New York
BWI	Baltimore, Washington
CCS	Caracas, Venezuela
CAI	Cairo, Egypt
CDG	Paris, France
CHI	Chicago, Illinois
CLE	Cleveland, Ohio
CPH	Copenhagen, Denmark
CUN	Cancun, Mexico
CVG	Cincinnati, Ohio
CLT	Charlotte, North Carolina
DEL	Delhi, India
DEN	Denver, Colorado
DTT	Detroit, Michigan
DFW	Dallas-Fort Worth, Texas
DIA	Denver, Colorado
DTW	Detroit, Michigan
DUB	Dublin, Ireland
DXB	Dubai, United Arab Emirates
EDI	Edinburgh, Scotland
ERW	Newark, New Jersey
FRA	Frankfurt, Germany
FPO	Freeport, Bahamas
GBE	Gaborone, Bostwana
GDL	Guadalajara, Mexico
GLA	Glasgow, Scotland
GUA	Guatemala City, Guatemala
GVA	Geneva, Switzerland
GYE	Guayaquil, Ecuador
HAM	Hamburg, Germany
HKG	Hong Kong
HNL	Honolulu, Hawaii

HRE	Harare, Zimbabwe
IAD	Washington, DC
IAH	Houston, Texas
IND	Indianapolis, Indiana
JFK	New York, NY (Kennedy)
JNB	Johannesburg, South Africa
KIN	Kingston, Jamaica
KUL	Kuala Lumpur, Malaysia
LAS	Las Vegas, Nevada
LAX	Los Angeles, California
LCA	Lamaca, Cyprus
LED	St. Petersburg, Russia
LGA	New York, NY (La Guardia)
LGW	Londo, England (Gatwick)
LHR	London, England (Heathrow)
LIM	Lima, Peru
LIS	Lisbon, Portugal
LIT	Little Rock, Arkansas
LPB	La Paz, Bolivia
MAD	Madrid, Spain
MAN	Manchester, England
MCI	Kansas City, Missouri
MCO	Orlando, Florida
MDW	Midway, Chicago, Illinois
MDZ	Mendoza, Argentina
MEL	Melbourne, Australia
MEX	Mexico City, Mexico
MIA	Miami, Florida
MID	Merida, Mexico
MIL	Milan, Italy
MKE	Milwaukee, Wisconsin
MNL	Manila, Philippines
MOW	Moscow, Russia
MSP	Minneapolis, Minnesota
MSY	New Orleans, Louisiana
MTY	Monterey, Mexico
MUC	Munich, Germany

MVD	Montevideo, Uruguay
NBO	Nairobi, Kenya
NYC	New York, New York
OAX	Oaxaca, Mexico
OGG	Maui, Hawaii
OKC	Oklahoma City, Oklahoma
OMA	Omaha, Nebraska
ORF	Norfolk, Virginia
ORL	Orlando, Florida
ORD	Chicago, Illinois (O'Hare)
ORY	Paris-Orly Airport, France
OSA	Osaka, Japan
PAC	Panama City, Panama
PBI	West Palm Beach, Florida
PEK	Beijing, China
PHL	Philadelphia, Pennsylvania
PHX	Phoenix, Arizona
PIT	Pittsburgh, Pennsylvania
PIE	St. Petersburg, Florida
POS	Port of Spain, Trinidad
PPT	Papeete, Tahiti
PRG	Prague, Czech Republic
PVR	Puerto Vallarta, Mexico
QHO	Houston, Texas
RIO	Rio de Janeiro, Brazil
ROM	Rome, Italy
RSW	Ft. Myers, Florida
SAN	San Diego, California
SAO	Sao Paulo, Brazil
SAT	San Antonio, Texas
SAV	Savannah, Georgia
SCL	Santiago, Chile
SDF	Louisville, Kentucky
SDQ	Santo Domingo, Dominican Republic
SEA	Seattle, Washington
SEL	Seoul, Korea
SFO	San Francisco, California

SGN	Saigon, Vietnam
SHA	Shanghai, China
SIN	Singapore
SJD	San Jose Cabo, Mexico
SJU	San Juan, Puerto Rico
SRQ	Sarasota, Florida
STL	St. Louis, Missouri
STO	Stockholm, Sweden
SYD	Sydney, Australia
TLV	Tel Aviv, Israel
TPA	Tampa, Florida
TPE	Taipei, Taiwan
TUL	Tulsa, Oklahoma
TUS	Tucson, Arizona
TYO	Tokyo, Japan
UIO	Quito, Ecuador
VIE	Vienna, Austria
WAS	Washington, DC
WAW	Warsaw, Poland
YMX	Montreal, Quebec
YVR	Vancouver, British Columbia
YYZ	Toronto, Ontario
ZRH	Zurich, Switzerland

Studio 4 Productions
ORDER FORM

QUANTITY

_____ *Airfare Secrets Exposed, 3rd ed.* @ $14.95 per copy   _____

The Case for Character Education

_____ paperback copies @ $11.95 per copy   _____

_____ hardcover copies @ $18.95 per copy   _____

_____ *Earthquake Prepared* @ $10.95 per copy   _____

_____ *Grandma Was Right!* @ $11.95 per copy   _____

_____ *If You have Kids, Then Be a Parent!* @ $4.95 per copy   _____

_____ *Seeing Beyond the Wrinkles, 2nd ed.* @ $12.95 per copy   _____

_____ *Shadowdad* @ $11.95 per copy   _____

_____ *Study Guide* @ $4.95 per copy   _____

_____ *To Grandma's House, We...Stay* @ $12.95 per copy   _____

California Residents add 8.25% tax   _____

Postage & Handling for one copy $2.50

Postage & Handling for additional copies @ 75¢ each   _____

TOTAL ENCLOSED   _____

PAYMENT TYPE

❑ Check   ❑ Money Order   Credit Card #: _____

❑ Mastercard   ❑ Visa

❑ Discover   ❑ American Express   Exp. Date: _____

Name: _____

Address: _____

City: _____ State: _____ Zip: _____

Make checks payable to Studio 4 Productions. Most orders ship within 24 hours of receipt. Please allow 1-2 weeks for delivery.

Studio 4 Productions
P.O. Box 280400
Northridge, CA 91328-0400
U.S.A.

(888) PUBLISH • (818) 700-2522
Fax: (818) 700-8666
www.studio4productions.com